Bruised, Broken and Blessed

Life Changing Stories That Will Ignite Hope, Elevate Personal Growth, and Confirm Your Greatness

Compiled by: Charron Monaye & Shontaye Hawkins, MPA

Foreword by: Brittany Garth

Compiled by Charron Monaye & Shontaye Hawkins, MPA

© 2018

ALL RIGHTS RESERVED. No part of this book may be reproduced in any written, electronic, recording, or photocopying without written permission of the publisher or author. The exception would be in the case of brief quotations embodied in the critical articles or reviews and pages where permission is specifically granted by the publisher or author.

PUBLISHED BY: Pen Legacy®, LLC.

DISCLAIMER

Although you may find the teachings, life lessons and examples in this book to be useful, the book is sold with the understanding that neither the co-authors nor Pen Legacy, LLC. are engaged in presenting any legal, relationship, financial, emotional, or health advice. Any person experiences, financial or goal concerns, or any anxiety, depression, health, or relationship issues, should consult with a licensed therapist, advisor, licensed psychologist, or any qualified professional before commencing into anything described in this book. This book's intent is to provide you with the writer's account and experience with overcoming life matters. All results will differ than yours; however, our goal is to provide you with our "take" on how to overcome and be resilient when faced with circumstances or issues. There are lessons in every blessing.

Library of Congress Cataloging – in- Publication Data has been applied for.

ISBN: 978-0-692-05537-3

PRINTED IN THE UNITED STATES OF AMERICA.

Table of Contents

Foreword By: Brittany Garth

Inspiration By: Rev. Paul Jones

Chapter 1	Sang Thi Duong	4

To Single Mothers Everywhere....You Got This Thing Called Life. I Promise

Chapter 2	Jasmine York Ball	16

Making it to the "Start Line"

Chapter 3	Michael Simmons	28

A Man of All Seasons

Chapter 4	Briana McKnight	38

P.U.S.H (Persist, Pray, Press On) Until Something Happens

Chapter 5	Ontaria Kim Wilson	46

A Dream Deferred

Chapter 6	Dennis LA White	58

Resilient in Hollywood

Chapter 7	Summer Fitch	68

Potholes in My Lawn

Chapter 8	Anissa Zabriskie	78
	The Wounds of Time Can Be Healed	
Chapter 9	Kenneth R. Nelson Jr.	86
	Against All Odds… A Story of Struggle and Beating the Odds	
Chapter 10	Roberta A. Albany	96
	My "Why" After Breast Cancer	
Chapter 11	Latisha Stephens	108
	Why Me God?	
Chapter 12	Carnell Poteat	122
	My August Angel	
Chapter 13	Tyressa Ty	134
	Forging through the "Fiyah"	
Notes		140
Compiled By: Charron Monaye & Shontaye Hawkins, MBA		150
Order Form		153

I Won't Complain

I've had some good days
I've had some hills to climb
I've had some weary days
And some sleepless nights
But when I look around
And I think things over
All of my good days
Out-weigh my bad days
I won't complain

Sometimes the clouds are low
I can hardly see the road
I ask a question, Lord
Lord, why so much pain?
But he knows what's best for me
Although my weary eyes
They can't see
So I'll just say thank you Lord
I won't complain

The Lord Has been so good to me
He's been good to me
More than this old world or you could ever be
He's been so good, To me
He dried all of my tears away
Turned my midnights into day
So I'll just say thank you Lord

~ Rev. Paul Jones

Foreword

Have you ever been broke? Not just financially broke, but emotionally and spiritually broken in a way that only hitting rock-bottom can make a change in your life for the better. I was broken in so many ways in my life that I didn't even know were possible. From broke bank accounts, broken relationships and broken edges, my life in 2014 was a far cry from the successful life coach people may view me as today. I was depressed, losing my hair and afraid. At this time period in my life, I was working as a program director at a non-profit agency and was informed by my employer that my staff and I would not be able to be paid until further notice; however we were still expected to attend work. 1 month turned into nearly 5 months of unpaid labor causing me to deplete my savings account and 90% of my staff. Have you ever gone to bed hungry? I remember on several occasions going to bed so angry about my situation that I no longer felt the hunger pains in my stomach caused from only eating dollar sliced bread for my one meal of the day. My pride led me down an uncomfortable road of keeping my financial situation a secret in hopes of "appearing" to have it all together. I gave my rock bottom lifestyle an eviction notice the same day I came home to my lights being cut off. I was months behind on paying my mortgage and facing homelessness and I was days away from having my car repossessed. I had officially had enough and after a long cry and conversation with God, I realized that my issue was not that I was broke; it was that I was being broken up in efforts to become the person God had created me to be. The struggle maybe real, but sometimes the struggle is necessary. 6 months from the day I discovered the purpose for my pain,

I launched a life coaching business dedicated to the empowerment of women that has allowed me the ability to work with hundreds of women from around the globe in 8 different countries and counting. Your future life does not have to resemble your current situation.

Life is about learning from our broken moments to be modeled into the true you! I welcome you to not only read the amazing stories shared throughout "Broken, Bruised and Blessed" but to actually be a witness in the power of different women and men sharing their "struggle story" in efforts to help you reach your next chapter in life for success. Your pain does not define you, your perception does.

Brittany Garth

Life Coach Brittany is an award winning ,international-certified women empowerment life coach who has provided services to women in over 7 different countries to include the US, The U.K, South Africa, China and more. In addition to being the owner of Dimensioned Wellness, founder of The DW Life Coach Network and an international motivational speaker and has been selected by Forbes Magazine as a top coach for the Forbes Coaches Council. Brittany has been selected by Cosmopolitan Magazine as one of their 50 social influencers for 2017 for their "Social Patrol" program. Brittany is a TEDx speaker, has spoken on "Global Entrepreneurship for Female Minorities" at Columbia University and has over 10 years of experience in the field of clinical based mental health for women and psycho-therapy.

Contact Info:
Brittany Garth
Website: www.dimensionedwellness.com
Email: info@dimensionedwellness.com
Facebook – https://m.facebook.com/dimensionedwellnessllc/
Instagram - dimensionedwellness
LinkedIn – Dimensioned Wellness

Your Blessing Is On The Other Side of this Page!!!

Sang Thi Duong

Sang Thi Duong is a communication & project strategist, speaker, and founder of the Single Mother Academy. She also holds the title of Ms. Missouri Universal 2018 where her platform is to empower Single Mothers to live their best life and defy societal stereotypes. She is blessed to work with her dream clients from all over the globe to help them take their millions of ideas and place them into an executable plan to connect and engage with their audience, increase revenue, and have ease of mind to sleep better at night. When she is not collaborating with a client or breaking barriers for Single Mothers, she can be found sipping on Starbucks, dancing for no reason, finding a reason to never cook, and just being a mom making a difference.

To Single Mothers Everywhere....

You Got This Thing Called Life. I Promise.

Dear Darling Single Mother,

Hello there. How are you? You good? I am so glad you are here reading this - and if you are not a Single Mother, you can read it too, after all, we are mothers. If you know a Single Mother, please share this letter with her too. I am here to spread love, joy, and happiness with a sprinkle of pleasure.

And before I dive deep into my letter, I want you to know that -- I got you. I hear you. I see you. I love you and this letter is for you.

You see, I have been a single mother for over 20 years, I have never been married and I believe in love like nobody's business. It wasn't until May 2015 that I began my journey of self-discovery, self-love, and what it meant to truly love myself unconditionally. And let me tell you, it has been the most joyous and pleasurable journey I have ever been on.

I am finally in a place of fully and utter love for myself. I love my body. I love my face. I love my stature as a mother. I love those who have wronged me. I love those who have been the source of my pain. I love life. I love who I have become and, deep down, I always knew I was this woman I am today. It was in my writings when I was younger, it was in my thoughts that I did not know how to nurture, and I craved this person I am my entire life.

You can become the person you are destined to be too. I know you can. It will take commitment, intention, and your attunement to your inner Goddess.

Now, I am going to take you on a short journey of my life prior to May 2015. Are you ready? Grab your favorite beverage, grab a cozy blanket, and let's become friends.

I graduated high school in 1996 with a basketball scholarship to a private college in Missouri. I wanted to get as far away from my parents as humanly possible. You see, the summer before my senior year, my mother betrayed me and that betrayal led to my father looking me in my face while he swung in his hammock smoking a cigarette that I was a disgrace to the family. And, again, that I would amount to nothing and to him, I was dead. And the only reason I was being allowed to stay at home was because the government said I had to.

So. On the following day of my graduation in May 1996, at 6AM, I left. I had nowhere to go. No money. No friends. Nothing. I was convinced to be a nanny to a young guy who lived with his father. This lasted only a few days as the father attempted to rape me and I fled.

Eventually I would live with my boss for the summer and I would meet a great guy. The great guy did not want me to leave for college because he wanted to be with me forever. At the time, I could not see past getting as far away from my parents as possible. And when August rolled around, I used ALL the money I had to go to college.

When I got to college, I had a $20 bill in my back pocket and no sheets for my bed. And the only things I had were in 2 cardboard boxes and a suitcase. That was it.

My first semester of college was TERRIBLE. My gpa was a .50. Yes you read that right a .50. Oh and about that basketball scholarship. My coach told me I was too fat to be on his team. I only weighed 150 lbs standing at 5'6" and I could box out like a boss. But that did not matter.

As I began my 2nd semester of college, I knew something had to change. So I decided I would go into the Air Force. I contacted the local recruiter, signed whatever papers I needed to sign. I mean, who was going to miss me. My parents were not speaking to me, I wasn't allowed to speak to my siblings -- the Air Force was a way to get an education, get paid, and be on a plan. Well, the the day I was supposed to travel to Kansas City to the do all my fancy testing...something happened. I felt weird. My boobs hurt ALOT.

I was pregnant.

I immediately called my recruiter and she told me what my options were. If I chose to have the baby, I would need to sign the rights to my baby over to someone while I was at camp and eventually I would be reunited OR if I chose not to have the baby, I would have to wait at least six weeks to do the physical testing and stuff.

I was torn.

How was I going to raise a baby? How did this happen? How could I have gotten myself into this situation. So I went to the father. He automatically said to get an abortion and he would pay for it. He already had a daughter and he did not want another child. BUT I was alone.

I chose to keep the baby. My son, Isaiah, was born October 1997 and I took him to class with me. I was determined to NOT be what society expected me to be as a single mother. All the odds were against me. And I do mean EVERY-THING!

I graduated college with Bachelor of Science in 3.5 years and my GPA was a 3.5. #SingleMomWinning

In April 2000, I found out I was pregnant again. Only this time, I was WITH the father - whom I was with since I was four months pregnant with my son. I was doing great things right? From the time he and I got together, it was full of ups and downs and all-arounds. For seven years, they were some great times and some super trying times. I suffered through years of physical, mental, and verbal abuse. And the worst part, I thought I did not deserve any better.

I mean, after all, my father was right. I was never going to amount to nothing. I WAS disgrace to the family and he reminded me of that when I graduated college in May 2000 when he "allowed" my mother to watch me walk across the stage.

For sake of timeline here, my daughter, Angel, was born in December 2000 and I went through postpartum depression (read my story here: Www.Sangtastik.com/true-story-why-i-didnt-touch-my-baby-for-3-months/) - and in August 2000, me, the kids, and her father would move to Chicago.

Long story super short - I left finally her dad in the Spring of 2003 and spent the next 6 months homeless. I had sent my kids to Texas to live with my sister and I lived out of my car. No one knew. It was terrible.

In January 2004, I moved into the suburbs of Chicago. Moved my kids back to me and was on a mission to start over and get my life together. And that moment happened when I was offered a job in Kansas City to work with the Social Security Administration. I took it and I went. I was a determined. I was committed to doing everything in my power to turn everything around. I had good health insurance for my kids, I was being paid well, I was blessed with a brand new car (since my car had been stolen on my first day in Missouri) and I was finally seeing a light at the end of my tunnel.

Until June 2005, I woke up to 175 missed calls from my sister, my brother, and my ex. What happened? My mother died unexpectedly in her sleep. My mother gone. My rekindled best friend. Just gone. I was 27 and experiencing death for the first time. I was devastated.

For the next 4 months, I was a zombie. I don't remember much of what happened during that time. Luckily, I had a boyfriend who took care of my kids during this time and he just let me be while trying to get me to live my life again. In October 2005, I just woke up one day and starting living. BUT there was one caveat. I was in denial that my mother was dead.

In the spring of 2006, my great boyfriend cheated on me again and I turned into a VERY BAD person. I became the abuser. I hurt him with words, I would throw things, and my anger was out of control. Anything would set me off. And my friends called me out on it a few times. But, again, I was in denial. He deserved it because he hurt me. Right?

I would eventually come to my sense in the fall of 2009. Yes, he took the abuse for years. I broke up with him and I told him I was not a good person for him and I no longer wanted to hurt him. He begged me not to leave. But, here's the deal. I had brainwashed to be this way. And I knew in my heart, I was doing what was best for him...and me.

In April 2010, my world would change again when the most romantic thing ever happened. I flew across the country to go on a date with a guy I had never met and he would change my life. Yet again!

I was finally with a guy whom I enjoyed having sex with and did not feel like I was an object, whom was not abusive to me verbally and physically, who was truly into protecting me as a woman -- and with any relationship. There were ups and downs and in May 2015 -- he left and I did not see him again until January 2017.

What happened during all that time? I grew. I became aware. I birthed my desires. I learned to love myself. I learned to trust women. I learned how to receive without resistance. I learned how my body spoke to me. I learned how to communicate with those around me in the most delightful way. I learned to use the power of daily pleasure to live a ridiculously amazing life.

Pleasure is a feeling of happy satisfaction. Not necessarily a sexual pleasure but it can be. *wink

And everyday I wake up, I desire to bring joy and inspiration to everyone who crosses my path. I use what pleasures me to light up the world with my magnetism. I know why I am on this earth and it is to help as many single mothers as I possibly can. When I had my first child, and I was faced with all those statistics -- I was determined to be in the lesser percentage. It has always been a burning desire within me to help others and it took me quite some time to get here.

I want to shorten your time. I want you to live your best life NOW. I want you to think beyond the parameters of what society has for you. I want to look fear in the eye and say I AM RELENTLESS. YOU WILL NOT STOP BE FROM LIVING A RIDICULOUSLY AMAZING LIFE.

Now. What I did not share was all the details in between AND the million emotions that came with every experience, every relationship, every job, every moment as a single mother. And I am here to tell you that every emotion that you have...is OK to have. Allow yourself to embody that emotion and one of my best tools to work emotions through my body -- dancing.

Need to feel sexy - play this song - Got It by Marian Hill

Need to feel your way through anger - play this song - Crazy In Love (Remix) by Beyonce

Need to a confidence boost - play this song - Me Too by Meghan Trainer

Need to just take a dance break - play this song - Cha Cha Slide by Casper

Because, I am here to tell you that everything you go through and every emotion you have is valid.

It's OK that you want to lose your mind and throw shoes at people.

It's OK when you want to be isolated and not speak to anyone.

It's OK when you feel the world has come crashing down and you want to take the day off.

It's OK to slam the door and yell at your kids for telling them to do something for the millionth time.

It's OK to go get a pedicure alone.

It's OK for the people to talk about you, what you buy, how you live your live because their opinions are none of your business. (this one is the hardest to learn)

It's OK to be different, go against the grain and defy the odds.

It's OK to want more, be more, and desire more.

It's OK for you to have lavish things too.

It's OK to go to a parent meeting feeling sexy.

It's OK to take long baths with candles and lock yourself in the bathroom.

It's OK to buy yourself something and NOT feel guilty.

Darling Single Mother. No matter what is going on in your life, I promise you. You are amazing. You are resilient. You are loved. You are the heartbeat of your family. You exude greatness more than you know - and your heart knows this.

I believe in you. You are beautiful inside and out. You are a Goddess. You deserve all the happiness the world has to offer. You deserve white roses. You deserve pleasure. You deserve everything you desire and then some.

And when your day is going in the worst possible way you feel known to man, I want you to know - You will survive. I know you will.

I have taken my son from cradle to college who played competitive sports his entire life. My daughter is a competitive dancer, high fashion model, is in the top 5% of her class and pushes me to my up level my greatness everyday. We have all three been through some tough times and with every challenge, I came out on top and I know you will too.

I read a book that was released in December 2017 by one of my all-time favorite writers and authors EVER. And I do mean EVER. The book is called, You're Going to Survive: True stories about adversity, rejection, defeat, terrible bosses, online trolls, 1-star Yelp reviews, and other soul-crushing experiences — and how to get through it by Alexandra Franzen. Look it up on Amazon. Order it. Read it. And if you have read this far, reach out to me and I will share a gift with you.

Now darling single mother, the journey you are on right now is unique to you. I want to listen to your story. I want to help you find what pleasures you and what brings you joy. I want you to BE the woman you desire to be.

Remember, I got you. I hear you. I see you. I love you and this letter is for you.

With glitter, gratitude, and so much love,

P.S. Want to listen to this story instead - go to www.soundcloud.com/mssangd - and find the story in audio there.

Jasmine York Ball

Jasmine York-Ball is a Freelance Writer and the Editor in Chief of BlackTie Magazine, a lifestyle magazine in Montgomery, AL from the African American perspective that she publishes alongside her husband Christopher Ball to spread awareness of minority owned businesses and the positive happenings occurring within our culture.

With an undergrad in Creative Writing and over 7 years in the publications industry, Jasmine uses her knowledge and experience as a content marketer to help entrepreneurs and small business owners communicate their message to their ideal clients and get the exposure they need to grow their business. Jasmine is an award-winning journalist with a certification in Inbound Marketing. She has served as the associate publisher of the fastest growing print media publication in all of North America, has written for several print and online media outlets throughout the nation, and has served as the lead writer over various content marketing campaigns for both large corporations and small business clients.

Jasmine is a small town girl from Selma, AL with a big life mission to use her writing to serve others and connect them to resources that will help them live more informed, inspired, and overall better lives.

IG: @jasminethewriter
Facebook/LinkedIn: Jasmine York Ball
Website: blacktiemontgomery.com

Making it to the "Start Line"

A PIVOTAL TURN

When I was thirteen, I remember sitting on the front steps of our porch one windless autumn evening thinking that my life was perfect. Granted, we were poor, on government assistance, and I was the youngest of six in a single parent household, but it was the little things that mattered. I had a good family and great friends throughout the neighborhood that all looked out for each other. It was truly a village. However, little did I know, the very next night after having that thought my reality soon shifted and life as I knew it suddenly changed forever.

I remember falling asleep on the couch and waking up in the middle of the night per usual. My mom had come in the living room where I was laying, but kept staring out of the front window. I remember the orange street lights beaming through the curtains as she pulled them back, casting a shadow of her silhouette on the wall of awards and certificates my older siblings and I got from school.

As hard as I tried to go to sleep, I kept wondering what was my mom staring at outside and what was on her mind that seemed to be worrying her in silence. Then just as my curiosity grew, she slowly crept her way over to where I laid, kneeled down, and began to "wake" me up.

"Jasmine," she said as she placed a wad of cash in my hand that came out to be maybe $40 or $60. "This is for you and Ashley. I'll be back in a couple of days."

She didn't say too much, but explained that she would be leaving my sister and I with our older brother, told me she loved me, then headed out the door. That was the first time I could remember her vocally expressing that she loved me, so in that moment I knew there must've been something serious going on that she wasn't mentioning.

That night I slept in a suspended curiosity, restless on one hand, and on the other hand, a little excited about having the house to ourselves. Our brother was pretty laid back and cool, so in my mind I considered being under his care as a newfound freedom.

However, that freedom was short-lived.

The very next morning after my mother left, I got called into the principal's office. I couldn't have been in my first period class for more than 20 or 30 minutes or so before hearing my name being called on the loud speaker to come down to the front office.

"This doesn't happen to me," I remember thinking. "Could I be in trouble?" It was just weird because I knew I hadn't done anything wrong and I just couldn't piece together why on earth I was being pulled out of class.

As I approached the office, I slowly opened the door at which point the secretary asked,

"Are you Jasmine York?"

"Yeah."

"Your mom says you're being withdrawn. Here's your paperwork. I need you to have all of your teachers sign this and you need to return all of your books."

"What? Where is she? Is she here?"

"No, she called in."

"May I use the phone?"

"Sure."

I was frantic. My heart pounded in my chest. I was suspended in the present moment, unsure of what the future held, unsure of what I might hear on the other end, but I was pissed and I needed answers. There was no way this was happening to me. Why in the world was she withdrawing me from school? Where was I even going? And why didn't she give me a heads up?

I called the house phone a few times, but no answer. So I called my neighbors who lived across the street to see if my mom's car was outside or to see if she was home. She was not.

"So what school are you going to," asked the secretary as I hung up the phone unsure of what to do next.

"I don't know," I said.

There was nothing more I could think to do other than to take the paperwork, drag myself back to class, and try not to cry from confusion, betrayal, or frustration. I just wanted to know what was going on, but with no way of reaching my mom, it was hopeless.

My mother showed up later that day to pick my sister and I up from school. But rather than informing us of the next school we'd be enrolling in, she alerted us that when we got home we were to pack our lives (or as much of it as we could pack in a few hours) before starting our lives over in a new city and a new state I'd never even visited that was 800 miles away.

I used to resent my mom for that day, especially since I didn't find out until later the reason why we moved so abruptly. As an adult I understand now that she did the best she could do in the sphere of awareness that she was in at the time. I'm also grateful because looking back I know that in order for me to expand my worldview, I needed to grow out of the small town mind and life that I had gotten so accustomed to over the years.

Months after we abruptly moved, my mom later disclosed to us that she suffered a near death experience from a stranger that followed her from work and had her at gunpoint. That encounter sparked the beginning of her paranoia, which eventually put a strain on our family's dynamic as it progressed over time. Years following, we found out she was declared as a paranoid schizophrenic.

THE POWER OF SELF-RELIANCE

I remember being a freshmen in college living within my oldest brother and his wife because our family got evicted, and at the time my single mother was homeless and eventually locked up in a mental institution.

It hurt my heart when our family got separated. I remember staring out the window anytime I sat in the passenger seat or the backseat, studying my surroundings, looking for my mom, not knowing where on earth she could've been or if she was okay.

It was through that stage of my life that I learned the power of self-reliance. I attended a private Christian college that was walking distance from where I lived. As a freshmen, I remember being frustrated with not having a car and not coming from a well-to-do "normal" family that lent or bought their kids cars. But as frustrated as I was about what I lacked, nothing in my reality changed until the agony inside of me grew and until I got so tired and fed up with the situation that I didn't wait for motivation to come. Instead I took action to create the change I wanted to see with a sense of urgency.

In addition to work study, I picked up two or three other gigs to help me save while I was enrolled in school full-time. I would wake up for my 7:00 a.m. class and wouldn't get home until after 9:00 p.m. most weekday nights. I stopped buying clothes and couldn't wait to throw my paycheck in my savings account. It took me 3 to 4 months to get car after I got "sick and tired or being sick and tired." I saved over $2,000 and paid cash for it outright. It was the best feeling in the world, having something of my very own.

Hitting that first big goal gave me the confidence and hunger to manifest more and more of the life I dreamed of living, so I didn't stop there. I quit complaining and started making decisions. I always had a subtle belief about myself that I *could* be successful, but it wasn't until that moment that I actually started to believe in myself enough to make the decision to be a co-creator of my own life rather than a victim.

In that moment, I believe God was teaching me that it wasn't about where I started from or if I was born with a handout or a leg up. It was about what I wanted to see for myself and what I was willing to sacrifice in order to get there. I learned the value of hard work and I began to understand that if I was going to "make it" in life, it was unrealistic of me to wait for someone else to make it easy for me or serve up the life of my dreams on a platter.

I learned that somewhere through it all, no matter what, if it wasn't a win, it was a lesson. As hard as lessons may have been sometimes, the bigger picture usually reminded me to look on the bright side because I understood that in essence, as long as God was with me I was going to be okay.

GAINING TRACTION THROUGH PERSERVERANCE

Through self-reliance, I developed an indescribable peace that no matter what unfolded in life, God was with me always and somehow everything would work together for good.

I was in school for creative writing, but at the time I wasn't sure what I wanted to do with the degree. All I knew was that I wanted to write and that I wanted to connect people to valuable information that would make a difference in their lives. I wasn't clear yet on what that looked like for me as it related to a dream job or dream title, but I was open to learning everything I could about the craft just to get better at it.

So with my newfound "get-it-for-yourself" mentality, while I was in college I began to get my hands involved in every single publication there was on campus: yearbook, newspaper, a magazine in the Bible department, the career newsletter, the creative writing department's publication, the school's website, and alumni magazine, etc.

I immersed myself in the industry just to learn more about the field. I spent almost every Friday in my writing mentor's office, picking his brain and learning everything he was willing to share about being a news reporter and careers as a writer.

My sophomore year I took my resume to the career services department at my college to do a mock interview and get feedback and advisement. The director looked over my resume, and although she thought it looked good, recommended that I broaden my experience outside of campus. She then gave me the contact information to a local magazine publisher, suggesting that I reach out to volunteer for the experience. When I got back to my computer, that's exactly what I did. I ended up getting called in for an interview, landed a 90 day internship, and eventually got hired on as a paid writer at the end of that internship – all before starting my junior year of college.

When the director advised me to broaden my experience outside of campus, I didn't stop with reaching out to her point of contact. I also reached out to several publications throughout the nation and started picking up gigs as a freelance writer and editor all over the southeast.

I also completed three internships and worked full time hours while being a full time student. I was promoted to editor for the various publications I contributed for on campus, and even took on a role as associate publisher for one of the fastest growing print media companies in all of North America – all before graduating college!

MAKING IT TO "THE START LINE"

When I landed the job as a paid writer for the magazine publisher, I fell in love with the industry and knew that no matter how I used my degree, I wanted to be tied to a magazine company in some form or fashion.

It wasn't until a few years after working there, and only after feeling like I reached my potential in the position I held, that I eventually ventured off to another company to once again broaden my writing experience. I then became the lead writer on the marketing team at a management company and added a certification in Inbound Marketing under my belt. While there, I created content marketing campaigns for big brands to include writing TV and radio commercials, direct mail campaigns, email marketing, business blogging, social media, and more.

It was through a combination of all of my work experience (and marrying my high school sweetheart Chris) that naturally moved me in the direction of using what I know about publications and content marketing to serve others through a business of my very own. Having multiple streams of income and being in business for myself became a next big goal that I wanted to achieve. Now as a Freelance Writer and Editor in Chief of a print magazine for African Americans (BlackTie Magazine), I take what I know about the writing and marketing industry to help entrepreneurs communicate their message to their ideal clients and get the exposure they need to grow their business.

Many people when they look at me or my life today, they often describe me as successful or say, "Wow, you're so lucky", without always knowing the journey and experiences I faced early on that molded me into being the type of business woman that I have to be today.

We all have different odds stacked up against us, and there are challenges and distractions we all face on a day to day. But with God, a passion, a vision, a plan, discipline, accountability, and a certain level of belief within yourself, I learned that you can achieve whatever "it" is you set out to do. The question is, how serious are you about having it with urgency and what are you willing to sacrifice in order to get it?

RUNNING YOUR RACE

People often ask me, "How did you do it?" or "What advice would you share to someone who's trying to get to where you are?" To answer that, I would say that we all have our own idea of what success looks like for us. For me, I know that I'm just getting started, but I have a list of goals and I stick to it. Every day I'm focused on becoming a better and better version of myself than I was yesterday.

Anyone seeking to understand, know this: Part of getting "there" wherever "there" is, is understanding that you are your own competition, and also realizing that the biggest goals anyone sets out to achieve usually will require that person to focus on being that thing rather than simply doing that thing to cross it off a to do list. Do you know what I mean? Allow me to explain.

What I've found is that when many people set a big goal, whether it's to lose 20 lbs., start a business, or publish a book, etc., they refer to achieving their goal as making it to the finish line. However, I say that with most of the big goals we set out to achieve, what we usually refer to as crossing the finish line is really the "start line" because the journey have just begun.

When you lose 20 lbs. you have to keep it off, when you start a business, you have to run it, and when you publish a book, you have to sell it, right? See where I'm going with this?

You see, most big goals we set out to achieve, in route to pursuing them becomes a lifestyle and begins to change us from the inside out. What I learned in my journey is that no matter where we come from or what advantages or disadvantages we may face, making it to the "start line" is half the battle. And once we are at that start line and hit our big goal, the task then becomes making the decision every day to win or lose and get up and run our race. Then at the end of every day when we go to bed, we cross the finish line.

Once we've hit our goal, the everyday struggle shifts to making it to our start line every day to run our race. There will always be a million and one thing going on around us that can distract us or keep us stuck in the same position we've been in for years.

That's why I stress the point of understanding that hitting that big goal is making it to the start line. Once you get it in your head that every day we have to run our own race, and at the end of the day, we all must cross the finish line, then you will feel more clearly the power of self-reliance and be able to lean on God in knowing that you are your own competition and how and when you cross the finish line is up to you. Run, walk, crawl, or pace yourself and jog. Make it a great day or not, the choice is yours.

Michael S. Simmons

Michael S. Simmons, Father and Retired Bus Operator from Septa, is a man of many passions, but a lover of the arts and music. Michael believes that in order to excel in life you must first believe that it is possible and then dare to be great. This belief has carried him for more than 70+ years. That's why it's hard to pinpoint exactly who he is, but very easy to know what he can do and capable of achieving. Mr. Simmons is a trained Gymnast, Dancer Martial Artist, and the Drummer. He was a dancer of modern, jazz and ballet for the Philadelphia Cotillion Sociality and Principal Dancer for Anna Branch and the Stephen Dancer's Revue and the Drummer for the 70's group, "Crosstown Traffic". He currently plays the drums for Morning Service at Ebenezer Baptist Church, in Philadelphia, PA.

With all of his training, traveling and success, Mr. Simmons's will tell anyone that his greatest accomplishment is making it to the Junior Olympics in February 1964, because he was the only black boy to make it at a time when African Americans were not allowed. Michael Simmons, a man who broke barriers, knocked down walls, and opened doors of opportunity that was deemed impossible.

A Man for All Seasons

They say we are called by God to be who it is that He wants us to be. Yet, in all of my seventy-four years of living, I'm still not sure what exactly His purpose is for me. You see, my passion is music and being a drummer; my love is family; and my pastime is watching television in the basement of my home. Still, in all of that, I have not found the answer to my question. *What and who was I called to be?* If you knew me back during my middle and high school years, you would have probably said I was ordained to be a gymnast. However, for me, being a gymnast was a gift that started from a humble beginning.

Back in the summer of 1957, while entertaining myself by tumbling on an old mattress in the schoolyard, Mr. Garfinkle approached me and asked if I would try out for the gym team. I took him up on his invitation and went inside to the gymnasium to sign up. However, upon entering the gym, I noticed all of the boys were wearing uniforms and sneakers. Embarrassed, I left and went back outside to the mattress to continue flipping. Afterwards, Mr. Garfinkle asked me if everything was okay. That's when I told him my reason for not signing up. I was too embarrassed because I couldn't afford the gym clothes and shoes needed to participate. Without saying another word, he took me home, met my parents, and told them that he would buy me a gym suit and a pair of sneakers in exchange for me joining the team. After my parents gave their permission, he turned to me and said something I will never forget.

"No matter how poor you think you are, there are many riches tucked away inside of you," he told me.

Mr. Garfinkle has since passed away, but his words have been and continue to be passed on as motivation for my children and those who are within my church and neighborhood. He was the first man to ever believe in me, and keeping my promise, I took the gym suit and sneakers he bought for me and started my journey toward becoming a gymnast. Without him, I wouldn't be the "man for all seasons" that I am today. Because of him, I have achieved so much, even though the odds were stacked against me.

Gymnastics Stats

1958 ~ Jr. High Championship (Second Place)
1959 ~ Sr. High Championship (Second Place)
1960 ~ Sr. High Championship (First Place)
1960 ~ Temple Invitational Championship (First Place)
1960 ~ YMCA Regional Championship (First Place)
1960 ~ Department of Recreation Championship (First Place)
1962 ~ Eastern Regional Champion
1962 ~ YMCA Regional Champion
1962 ~ Philadelphia Department of Recreation Champion
1963 ~ Philadelphia Department of Recreation Champion
1964 ~ Jr. Olympic National Champion

In addition to Mr. Garfinkle, there was another man who helped me become one of the biggest names in the field of gymnastics. Mr. Raymond Coleman taught me and helped me master one move that would take me from being an amateur to championship worthy.

In 1957, I met Mr. Coleman in the night gym at Vaux Middle School, where he was doing a maneuver I thought people only did on television...a back handspring. I don't think he realized by me watching him and seeing how I could perfect that move, it would make me the king of the gymnastics circuit, and it did!

During my time of learning and practicing, I became the captain of the gymnastic team and began my reign of wins by taking second place in the city-wide public championships. My success in gymnastics did not stop when I left Vaux; it heightened in my years at Thomas Edison Senior High School. After seeing the competition on the high school level, I became devoted to the sport, training for six hours every day. I had found my niche and discovered my gift. My rigorous training led to me placing second at the 1959 Senior High Championships, but even though I placed second, it still felt like losing to me. So, my desire to be the best increased. In addition, during this time with civil rights and race relations, losing to a Caucasian was not how I wanted to be remembered. So, I made it my mission to never stand below them on the podium again.

Even though the season ended in February, my training did not. Matter of fact, it became more intense. My life consisted of going to school, training, eating, and sleeping! Anything worth having is worth fighting for, right? So, I fought! I fought with myself to be the best gymnast I could be. Plus, I met a young woman by the name of Cora Bass, who challenged me to do the impossible – win all major meets in gymnastics that I competed in. With my own personal determination and, now, her support behind me, I made a vow that I would not lose.

The next season, I returned to the gym with the mindset of *winning* first place at all regional school competitions. That motivation worked, because not only did I place first at the school championship, but also the Temple University Invitational Meet and Department of Recreation Meet. Needless to say, I felt like I was sitting on top of the world. This black boy dared to be great and my accomplishments proved I deserved nothing but *Gold*!

However, my time doing flips, handstands, and leaps had to be put on hold when I dropped out of high school and enlisted in the United States Army in order to provide for me and my sister while we were in the care of our foster mother. What I thought would provide a better life for my youngest sister and I became my biggest regret. I bought into what they sold, only to end up living in the most segregated place ever. Restricted in almost everything, I went back to my love for music and joined the Army's marching band as a drummer, while still holding onto my dream of winning Gold in the Olympics.

While home on leave, a mutual friend introduced me to a woman by the name of Katherine, who turned me on to the arts, mainly classical music and dance. I took a major interest in the two. However, being in the military, I could not fully indulge. But, while home on another leave, my sister Patricia, who I affectionately refer to as Pat, had a recital performance coming up at Moylan Recreation Center. Unfortunately, her boyfriend, John Payne, could not partner with her to perform the Waltz because he was having trouble learning the dance. So, Pat asked me to be her partner and together we performed. Based on that performance, my talent was recognized and I was offered the opportunity to perform with the Philadelphia Cotillion Society, where we went to New York under the tutelage of Anna Branch.

Being an athletic and drummer, I possessed the flexibility and understanding of rhythm to perform the dance routines effortlessly. But then, in 1962, an opportunity presented itself, and I put everything on the back burner. It was time for me to get my Gold.

It was National's time. This was my stepping stone to the Olympics. My time had arrived, and I was ready to claim my victory. I went on to win the Nationals and then the Junior Olympics. Next stop, the Olympics. All I had to do was make it to the next three gymnastic meets and then try out for the Olympics. Who would've thought a little black boy in foster care and living in the projects would be only three meets away from the Olympic tryouts? Then, the unthinkable happened.

I could not get anybody to sponsor me because I had no college experience, and with my last name being Simmons, it signified I was not Caucasian. Think that about. The *best*, the *champion*, a young man's dream broken all because he was black. In that moment, despite all of my awards, medals, and honors, Michael Simmons, the gymnast, was no more.

So, during the year 1964, I gained and lost what I had worked so hard for…a chance to go to the Olympics. Instead of drowning in my pain, though, I realized one denial doesn't stop no show. However, it can end a legacy. Still having a desire to grow within my athletic ability, I learned and later taught martial arts at Moylan Recreation Center, becoming the only African American to teach it during that time. I studied under Master Monsoo Park, who later became the choreographer of the movies *Fist of Fury* and *Enter the Dragon*. Through his teachings, I received a third-degree brown belt and became an instructor. Also in the year 1964, I was chosen to perform during the Philadelphia Eagles halftime show at Franklin Field. Not only was it an honor, but a self-esteem booster, as well. Especially with having had my dreams of being an Olympic gold medalist extinguished only a year prior. I can remember that day so clearly. The stadium was packed, the TV cameras were running, and I finally had my platform to win while still being a black man. This opportunity solidified that getting a "no" in gymnastics does not mean a "no" to everything else that life has to offer.

After that experience, I decided it was time for me to get serious about something else. Thus far, I was a gymnast, dancer, and martial artist. So what was left for me to do? I picked up my drumsticks and became the drummer I was while in the military. Those drumsticks never replaced my love of doing cartwheels, double back somersaults, full-twisting back somersaults, side somersaults, front somersaults with a half twist, and my signature handspring, but they were the vessel that has provided me with my legacy in life.

Music became my peace and passion; it still is. Playing the drums was the way I immersed in my passion. If you know and love music, then you know the drums carry the beat, provide the bass, and add life to any track, vocalist, and dancer. It is the instrument that controls what you hear versus what you feel, which, for me, gave me the satisfaction of feeling like a winner. Since I could no longer shine on the gym mat, I took my passion and shined on stage.

In 1968, I founded the group The James Boys. Then, in 1972, we changed the name of the group to Storm, and yet again, in 1973 the group underwent another name change to Evil. In 1975, we became known as Crosstown Traffic. To reignite my love for dance, I reconnected with Pat, who was performing with the Stephen Dancers, and made them a part of the Crosstown Traffic movement. We typically played at cabarets and the tristate club circuit, but we were also featured on television shows, *Around The Town* on Channel 12 and *City Lights* on Channel 3 and performed in Montreal, Canada. Then in June of 1976, Crosstown Traffic, along with the Stephen Dancers, had the privilege of being the opening act for the Godfather of Soul, James Brown during his performance in Albany, Georgia. In 1982, Crosstown Traffic dissolved, but I held on to my love of music by becoming a music collector and making CD's for people. To this day, I still own vinyl records and cassettes, and I make CD compilations for those who like to use music to help them reminisce back to the good ole days. In addition, I still play the drums, but now, it's for the Lord at Ebenezer Baptist Church.

Through music, I have been able to pass down my legacy to my children, grandchildren, and great-grandchildren. Out of everything I have accomplished in life, this has been the biggest blessing. Being able to watch my children engrossed in the music they heard during my band's rehearsal in the basement was a gift. Then to teach my daughters the dances of the '50s, '60s, and '70s, only to now have them out dance me, was always a treat when we went to different events. To showboat and showoff is what we do. To now be able to show my grandsons how to play the drums makes every loss, denial, and delay worth it. I can't honestly say I don't think about what life could have been if I would have been able to compete in and win the Olympics, but without that experience, life has still been one that I have enjoyed living. As I always say, this world owes me nothing, and on July 10, 2018, when I turn seventy-five, I'll be able to sit back, reminisce, and now read this book while reminding myself just how far I've come.

Sometimes in life, we can set our minds and hearts on something that may not serve us the rewards we expect later. That's not to say it was not for us, but rather it could have been there to propel you to what is. For me, my love for gymnastics was bigger than life itself, but when my ultimate goal was denied, I had to learn the lesson and not wallow in the pain. The gymnastic experience prepared me for what would occur later in my life as a drummer, husband, father, employee, significant other, and just an overall fun guy. It proved that no matter how hard we fight to win in life, we will almost always fall short somewhere down the road. I have not always been the best at everything, but knowing that I gave my best is all I need. Success is not what you make it, but what you get out of it.

Briana McKnight

Briana McKnight is a recent Graduate of Widener University where she received her BS in Finance with a minor in Accounting. During her time at Widener, she was a full time Student/Athlete, a leader on and off the Women's Indoor and Outdoor Track & Field Team. Briana spent time serving her community as a Student Ambassador, mentoring high school freshmen and incoming Business Majors. After graduation, Briana began her Professional career in the financial service industry as a financial control analyst for J.P. Morgan Chase. She is pursuing her designation as a Certified Management Accountant and is currently embarking on her journey as an entrepreneur.

P.U.S.H
(Persist, Pray, Press On) Until Something Happens

I am twenty two years old. I graduated college early, and am currently employed by THE largest investment bank in the world. I am actively pursuing my Management Accountant Designation, and now I'm an Author. Sounds pretty golden, right? I'd say so myself but all I can say is "I'm so glad troubles don't last always". My trouble was not my surroundings, was not my situations, and was not my path, it was ME and I didn't even know it. I went through the same things families go through everyday, but I struggled.

The thing is, I am a "do-er". As a child, instead of going outside to play, I challenged myself to read chapter books in less than a day or two or to beat 2 levels of my SIMS game before I could go on to do anything else. I handled my business, I put my head down and I got stuff done. This is the number one reason why I did so well in school. I was never the smartest kid in the room, but I was ALWAYS had an awesome GPA & great exam scores because I ALWAYS put my work in. I was/am focused, always thinking about the next step, the next best thing. Gracias to my Ma for the structure! You see, my life has always been structured. It has always been my pop pop, my mom, and I. I spent lots of time of extended family, I was shown SO much love & fun, but when I was 13, my structured life became a life of chaos.

When I was 12, my mom told me that she was pregnant. [What. The. F*$#]. It was bad enough that she was dating. She already had everything she needed in life (ME) LOL why would you have another baby? I was at my aunt's house when she came by to tell me. I was playing with my cousins when she called me outside. I am pretty sure my response was something like "oh okay" before I turned around to go back inside. I don't think I felt anything. I soon go over that. My brother is one of my biggest heartbeats.

But that wasn't what really threw me off balance. We moved. The house I grew up in, the house my mom grew up in, we left. My new home was a two-bedroom townhouse. It was a nice place. The first year was cool with my new family. My mom was happy; my step dad was friendly & cool. My brother was cute. But then we moved again the next year. This times a townhouse with 3 bedrooms. I could tell my parents weren't seeing eye-to-eye but I was too caught up in middle school woes to understand what was happening, but things became prevalent when my stepdad lost his job. Tensions were a lot higher, arguments were always taken place but we always seemed to make it back to our happy place. I believe I was about 15 when the eviction notice came. I asked my mom what is was and she explained to me what it meant. My mom & I have a very open relationship. She always made sure that I was aware and understood. If you don't learn from your mistakes, what's the point right?

Anyway, you guess it. It was time to move AGAIN. This time, back to my home. Pop Pop's house. My safe haven! Except when we got there, it wasn't the same. 2 years out made a difference. The house was a mess. Pop Pop was getting old, but we made it work. Tensions were still getting worse between my parents as they were back living under the roof of a parent and we only made it a year before they decided to move again. The new place was a two bedroom apartment in a smaller section of my school district; Me, my mom, my step dad, and my brother... in a two-bedroom apartment – Yes - We lived there for a year before my mom and step dad decided to call it quits. So there it was - My mom & I living on our own with my then 3 year-old, severely asthmatic brother, struggling to make things work financially. From age 15-18, I was helping my mom at home, working a part-time job on the weekends, playing volleyball in the Fall, running track in the Winter/Spring, spending nights in the ER with my brother, caught in the middle of relationship drama, participating in various extra-curricular activities in school, all while getting good grades. Structured, right? NOT.

I was functioning and performing well in school, but very few people know what I was dealing with on the inside. I was tired, broken, confused, hurt, and anxious ... all of the time. The littlest things would make me cry, irritable, and mean. I dropped 15 pounds caused by stress and could not put it back on for the life of me. I weighed about 100lbs soaking wet during my first two years of high school. I wasn't eating well. My mom sent me to a therapist for about 3 months. It worked for a while, but then I stopped going.

And like the old saying goes, "when it rains it pours". If being a nomad and dealing with messy divorces wasn't enough, grief had to get me. I was 16 when my Uncle Ricky passed away. He was my mom's older brother and my Godfather. I spent more with him and his family than I did anyone else growing up. He called me his 5th kid. His children were my siblings, even if they didn't want me around. His sudden death hurt. A year and a half later, the night before my college orientation, my Uncle Bryant passed away. He was the older brother to both my mom and my Uncle Ricky. He lived with me a short while at Pop Pop's house. He walked me to the bus stop every morning and picked me up every afternoon during my middle school career (Even though I had been doing it for years on my own and was more than capable of doing it myself). My biological father and I didn't have the best relationship growing up so my uncles took pride in me. I had more father figures that anyone could imagine, and in a blink of an eye, two of them were gone. Dealing with the death of two sons, my Pop Pop's heath began to decline quickly. He was diagnosed with colon cancer during my freshman year of college. My Pop Pop, my God given solace, the man, the myth, and the legend! Seeing him go through that pain hurt me, a lot.

Grief! It's an experience, a traumatic event. It's everything you hoped it wouldn't be. But it's inevitable. As some point, you have to will always have to come to the terms that you are forced to live without someone you love deeply. It happens in many forms. I was grieving people close to me who had passed away, and grieving the loss of support system for someone who has lost someone close to them, and grieving the loss of someone who is still alive but just out of your life.. Due to my already anxious nature, grief didn't help. I felt any and everything. Everyday was a struggle. The point is ... grief is a part of life that can tear you away. Some people feel a lot longer. Due to my already anxious nature, grief didn't help. Feelings don't come and go that easily. Some people feel a lot more than others. Some people feel a lot longer. I felt any and everything. Everyday was a struggle. I was depressed, but I was able to lead a functional life. I attest that to my athletics. My sports were my now therapy. I ran and worked out daily while my teammates kept me afloat. I don't even know if they knew what I was dealing with on the inside. But I got through.

Like, I mentioned before my trouble was not my surroundings, was not my situations, and was not my path, it was ME and I didn't even know it. I went through the same things families go through everyday, but I struggled. Parents get divorced. People move all of the time. People also deal with the loss of loved ones on a daily. But these things made me develop anxiety and these things made me develop functional depression. It is an ongoing struggle today. I could always handle my life. I was always "good" but I wasn't. I know what it feels like to have everything be okay but you just don't feel "okay". I know what it feels like to feel tremors through your entire body ... for what? I don't know. Like Mark Twain mentions, *"I've suffered a great many catastrophes in my life. Most of them never happened."*

I share my story with you to tell you encourage you to take care of YOU. Make sure that you not only achieve your professional goals, but to make sure your mental is right also. I am currently doing so in my newly published reflection journal "Boss Moves Start with You". Understand that you are not what happened to you and that you are not what people tell you that you are. You are who you want and choose to be. You are stronger than you think. You can overcome your pain. You can overcome your fear. You can bloom where you are planted. Whatever you are going through will pass. If you want to RISE, you will. Have faith, be present, and keep pushing. You are your only limit.

Ontaria Kim Wilson

With a passion for the arts, Ontaria Kim Wilson lives her life dedicated to creating and sharing her art. She is an accomplished dancer, choreographer, actress, writer and theater arts professional who has 26 years in the entertainment business. She has to her credit the following accomplishments: member of 3 distinguished dance companies; appeared as an actress, writer, or director in over 17 theatrical productions; 3 featured films; over 15 dancing placements in celebrity performances and written and co-written featured films and an animated television cartoon series.

Due to her extensive background she has taught and coached children and adults throughout the Delaware Valley (Pennsylvania, New Jersey, and Delaware) in the area of performing arts in elementary schools, spiritual institutions, community centers and performing arts schools. Her mantra is based on pouring into others so that the arts continue to thrive.

Ontaria believes that, "following your passion is the source of your success". Her passion has led her to be sought after internationally as well. In 2018, she will be starting a co-operation with the kingdom of Bahrain's 7TH Wave Performing Arts School as a guest facilitator and performer. Look forward to more works in the near future.

Contact Info:
Email: ceo.ontariawilson@gmail.com
Facebook: @ontariakimwilson
Instagram: @ontariakimwilson
Twitter: @ontariakimwilsn
Linkedin: Ontaria Kim Wilson

A Dream Deferred

The moment those doors opened I knew it was going down. I heard our music start and immediately those multicolored butterflies began their fluttering in the holler of my stomach leaving me torn between running into the bathroom or jumping into my cousin Florence's arms for safety. Those heavy brown doors swung open. The organist played like she was Little Richard's Aunty and I knew this was my moment. I started marching down the aisle, arms swinging to the choreographed steps of our youth ushers ministry, and all I heard was the music, the congregation belting my name, and my heart beating through my chest. That was the longest walk this five year old experienced in her lifetime but I loved every minute of it. I had been practicing every day. Soul Train was my drug and those cool dancers were the ingredients that kept me wanting more. I promised myself I'd be on Soul Train one day. Yup, just like the pointer sisters when they performed their song "Fire". You couldn't tell me I wasn't putting on my debut at Oak Grove Baptist Church. This performance confirmed my desire to perform.

I have always been full of dreams but I always depended on someone else to make those dreams come true. Asking for permission is what I've done since I can remember. "Mom, can I go to dance school?"; "Mom, can I go to gymnastics school?"; "Mom, can I...?" The answer(s) was consistent. I eventually took no for the answer and somehow found other things to occupy my time or concocted an adolescent remedy or alternative to the "No" but still remained a dreamer none the less. For example, in third grade my school had one free dance class. Can you guess what it was? If you answered ballet, modern, hip hop, African, or tap you are absolutely....WRONG! OK I'll give you a hint. It was a European style of dance that required a lot of skipping, jumping, and holding hands as your upper torso froze in the upright position. Have you guessed it yet? OK...I'll tell you... This African American girl with a jerry curl and braces learned how to do Irish Step. Yes I did! I was determined because where there is a will there is a way. Like Malcolm said, "By any means necessary". I had to quench my thirst for performance some way shape or form. So, by day I was Irish stepping at Good Shepherd Elementary school; but at night and on the weekends I was a B-Girl (One of Southwest Philly's Finest). Card board boxes, painter caps, kangaroo sneakers, cut out gloves, and boom boxes were my uniform. My dance name was K-Love. I was the youngest dancer and choreographer in my crew. What I didn't realize was that Street Dance/ Hip Hop would shape my life.

So, let's fast forward about 20 years. I had my first professional dance experience with the international hip hop theatre company Rennie Harris Pure Movement in 1992. This groundbreaking company was the brain child of Dr. Rennie Harris. In a male dominated company I was one of few females to become a long term company member. I stayed with the company for six years. I left because I was afforded the opportunity to choreograph and tour with R and B recording Artist Gina Thompson. It was kind of cool to walk into an audition room full of trained ballet and modern dancers and be the only hip hop dancer. As they executed their plies and tendus I skillfully executed my jumping jacks and lunges in my baggy pants, sweat suit jacket, and adidas. To be honest, I was nervous as hell. Why was I nervous? Well, a few years prior my best friend Anisa and I auditioned for the Philadelphia 76ers. We were ready and confident that we were going to make the cut. I showed up in my speedo bathing suit ready to showcase my body and dance skills. Out of 500 young ladies we made it to the final 70 dancers. Then came the final round. It was do or die. The choreography started and I felt like I was in an episode of Star Wars. The dancers started flipping and spinning in the air and when I realized that I was about to be eliminated I took it to the street and started popping, locking, and breakdancing. I was not going out without a fight. Two things happened that day. I realized that I had a lot to learn and I realized that I was good at what I do even in what seemed to be a fail. So, to walk into another audition where I clearly was not like everyone else I was overcome with a light blanket of fear. So, my number was called. I walked in to the room with Gina Thompson, her manager, and her dancer Kendra sitting at a table. I introduced myself, handed over my music. They started my cd and I released every move I had perfected. In the middle of my piece Gina stopped the music and stated, "That's what the ---I'm talking 'bout! Audition over! You're coming with me!" In that moment the eyes of the other dancers were rolling, faces were frowning. You would have thought I was public enemy number 1. Nevertheless, that was the beginning of my tour life. Remember that dream of being on Soul Train? Well, it came true. I wasn't a Pointer Sister or one of those hopeful dancers wishing the camera zoomed in on them while executing their best moves. I was a background dancer for Eve (Ruff Ryder's First Lady). Not only did I live my dream of being on Soul Train but I had a few more perks: Showtime At The Apollo (No sand man or boos from the audience); Late Night With Conan O'Brien; NFL Under The Helmet; Motown Live; Top Notch Hotels; the life. Next up to bat was Teddy Pendergrass. "Turn off the lights…and light a candle…" Yes, The legendary Teddy Bear himself. I toured with Teddy for two years and performed his last recorded performance "From Teddy with Love". My mom during that time was very supportive but she always pressed upon me to maintain a "REAL JOB." She always wanted me to make sure my absences from my full time job at Universal Atlantic Systems where I was the assistant to the chief engineer would not endanger my employment. Even though they supported my endeavors she always thought I was taking a risk. Her "no" transferred into doubts of prosperity for me in the world of art and entertainment. How do you contend with doubt from the outside when you're inner self is struggling to walk in faith and what you know you were called to be? My way of contending was by working a 9-5 and still holding on to my why. My "why" would later be challenged by religious leaders and my peers. I had become the director of the dance ministry at the church I was attending in 1999. About a year into being in leadership I was called into a meeting with the deacon board. This meeting was similar to an interrogation. First, they ran down those things they believed I was excelling in like tithing, making meetings, ministry growth, and skill in teaching. However, their motive was established as the chairman of the deacon board took the floor. "Sister Kim. You know we love you." I thought to myself, "what love got to do wit' this?" He continued, "…and know that this is all being in done in love. We need you here more. Now, we know you go on tour and you work with the gospel group and everything but we need you here." So I politely told him, "Deacon, with all due respect I will not stop working outside of this church. I will not stop touring. So, if I have to make a choice between leading a ministry within these four walls or going on tour than I choose the latter."

Well, the entire room grew quiet and one of the deacons inconspicuously gave me a thumbs up and a nod of approval. Eyebrows were raising, throats were clearing, swivel chairs were shifting, and egos had been dashed. Apologetically he responded with sincerity and conviction because he realized he was asking me to give up the passion and call that God placed over my life. Again, someone else was trying to guide my path without understanding who I was and what was required of me in order to become the "ME" I was supposed to be.

Interestingly enough, my mother's voice always rang in my mind. Each time I thought of pursuing my career in the arts full time I would hear both my mother and grandmother's voices say, "Don't you leave that job unless you have another one lined up." Well, I already knew what I wanted to line up but all of those missed opportunities and not being on the scene caused my line up to become just dreams deferred. My last tour was with Teddy Pendergrass in 2002. Unfortunately it was during the time when he fell sick and eventually passed away. This was technically the end to my tour life. I gave 100 percent to the company I worked for at the time. I worked with a local choir and began consulting dance ministries throughout Philadelphia but the arts became secondary. I eventually got a job working for University of Pennsylvania Hospital's Department of Radiation Oncology. During that time I considered becoming a nurse even though I hated the sight of blood, I suffered from acute empathy that would take over my body physically, and I couldn't stand the smell of hospitals but if I was going to be there I mind as well get all I can get out of the experience. However, everyone that had an opportunity to get to know me would ask, "Why are you here?" My response was always the same. I would shrug my shoulders, poke out my lips, raise my left eyebrow, let out a long sigh and say, "I don't know…I guess I'm here for the meantime." At 30 something I was still dancing around at the nurses' station, up and down the halls, through my doctor's office spaces, sitting in meetings changing every physician and leadership team member into a character, daydreaming about seeing my choreography and work on TV. Y'all, I was going crazy. Not only was I going crazy but I was making myself sick and I didn't know. I acquired bicep tendonitis, hair loss, and hypertension…a whopping 170/90. Yup, I was killing myself over other people's business, lives, and sacrificing my passion for what some would call "stability". Nonetheless I went to my primary doctor and he prescribed blood pressure medication. The day it was prescribed I took my first dose. I woke up from my sleep that evening to the room spinning. I was sweating profusely and urgently trying to wake my fiancée with acutely slurred speech. I finally mustered up enough strength to bang on the bathroom wall. He ran in and found me slumping over the tub. He dressed me and rushed me to University of

Pennsylvania's emergency room. My blood pressure had dropped to 60/40. If I were left alone a few minutes longer I would have died. While laying on my hospital bed I realized that if I didn't pursue my dreams I would literally die in my comfort zone and in a place where other's thought I should be. So, I made up my mind that I was going to leave. April 2013, I resigned from University of Pennsylvania Hospital. I didn't have "that job lined up" like my mom and grandmother advised. I had no idea how all of this would pan out. I forgot to mention that I didn't tell my mom that I was resigning until the week before my last day.

Why didn't I tell her? I didn't tell her because I had finally given myself permission. Permission to pursue the dreams God downloaded into my being. I came to the realization that I was responsible for the manifestation of my dreams. I had to do the work in order for that crazy faith to have measured results. My life now depended on my radical paradigm shift. No longer was I an employee. I had to work my business. I had to work my business like I worked for everyone else. Was it easy? No! Is it easy? No! I even questioned if I'd be able to resurface after years of being absent from main stream entertainment. Who would remember me? Who could I contact to let them know I was still around? How could I compete with the twenty something dancers since thirty and over is considered old in the dance world? The questions and doubt crept into my mind. But all the bible reading, purpose driven life speaking, believing in miracles, and praying was now put to the test and I had to walk in what I said I believed. Things like "GREATER IS HE THAT IS IN ME THEN HE THAT IS IN THE WORLD." I now understood the "Greater" was in me the entire time and I didn't behold it. I was not walking in the POWER that was in me. Truth be told, most of us don't walk in the power that is in us because we have been trained to seek approval and reward from others before we approve ourselves. That's what took me so long to realize that it was ok for me to give myself permission to walk in who God created me to be. And when I gave myself permission I created my exit. I created and wrote my first stage play "The Healing". My first theatre production sold out three days in row. From there I wrote, directed, and produced my second play "Detox" which was also a success. Not only did these new gifts surface. but I took on many actor, director, and choreographer roles in productions. My last play to date was Japanese Azteroids, which I co-wrote and directed. This production featured Darrin Henson and Jackie Christie (Basket Ball Wives of LA). Did I resurrect in the way I thought I would? Absolutely not! I never dreamed of writing or directing plays but life has a way of surprising you. Playwriting has even propelled me into writing for television and film. At this point in my life the sky isn't the limit.

So that five year old girl is a now forty something year old women. A woman with decades of no's and I don't think so tattooed on the walls of her life. But they are only there as fuel for her to keep creating the life and the legacy that she was destined to create. In the beginning God created a girl. She was trying to find herself but she was empty. The spirit of God hovered over her the entire time but she didn't know it until one day she was illuminated and no longer in the state in which she was originally.

Today I stand Once Bruised by the blows life can throw; broken by the words and experiences that cause the heart and mind to grow sick; but I am now Blessed beyond measure with knowing that I am who God called me to be and that my legacy is shaped by my ability to walk in the power within. And hey....Ain't No Stopping Me Now!

Dennis LA White

Dennis L.A. White is an American stage and screen actor noted for portraying Damion 'D-Roc' Butler in the Notorious B.I.G. biopic, Notorious.

Born and raised in southern California to a musician Mother and a military Father, Dennis was exposed to many different cultures and ideas. When his family relocated to Fayetteville, North Carolina he developed his love for music and acting. He was offered several scholarships to play baseball but he decided to take an academic scholarship at WSSU in North Carolina. In, 2001, Dennis, under the guise of "Dennis Da Menace", put out his Billboard charted album, "The Wonderful World of Dennis". In 2003, Dennis became the 1st African-American host at Fuse Television. He began to host several TV shows, "Weekend Vibe, HBO's 5 Rounds & Chatzone and MTV's "Hip Hop Life". He then pursued his love for acting with appearances in "The Brave One" with Jodie Foster, Law & Order: SVU, The Jury, "I Think I Love My Wife", Secrets, etc.
In 2009, Dennis created "Act Like You Know", a company

that gives acting workshops and seminars to aspiring Actors across the country. In 2009, Dennis became the character "Mistah Ray" on NBC's "Parenthood". In 2013, Dennis started a foundation called "M.O.R.P.H." to help rid racial profiling. More recently, you can see Dennis in FX's hit series "Atlanta" and TvOne's film, "Bad Dad Rehab". In 2017, he starred in a Steven Spielberg's film about PTSD called "Thank You For Your Service".

Contact Info:
Website: www.actlikeyouknow.org
Email: actlikeyouknowworkshops@gmail.com

Resilient in Hollywood

As an actor, Hollywood has bruised me. It exposed those that were jealous of my success and prayed for my downfall. It tried to break me by continuously telling me that I'm not good enough, attractive enough, or smart enough to make it. Yet, I stand here blessed because I am assured No Weapon Formed Against Me Shall Prosper. Plus, I know God has great things in store for me that no man can deter.

Never did I consider giving up at any point in my career. However, I must admit being an actor is a very challenging and lonely career choice. Several times it felt as though the walls were caving in on me. There were times when I couldn't see a direct path to success. I always knew it was there, but the roadblocks seemed to obstruct my vision. I fought through them, though. For instance, take the time when the head of Dark Gable, a music label I was signed to, died unexpectedly. Not only was it unfortunate that he passed, but his death occurred the day before our meeting with Sony Music, who were going to sign us to a deal. That destroyed any future we had with the project or my contract with Sony. I was distraught, depressed, and confused. I didn't know if I wanted to pursue music anymore. Especially since this happened around the time when there were a lot of "issues" arising between some of the major figures in the industry. Nobody had time to entertain "new opportunity" because they were trying to save their careers, lives, and images. Where did that leave me? The loss of that opportunity led me to focus more on my acting career.

Despite my loss in music, I refused to stay comfortable in my new reality. So, I channeled my all into my acting career. I became so focused on being successful that I could not lose. Even though I did hear "no" and "not right now" quite often, I received the right "yes's" from casting directing and executives because my acting gave me more exposure than I had previously while in the music industry. I can remember going to my first audition for a film called "Swimming". I traveled to Myrtle Beach (stole my mother's car to get there) and walked in the room with so much confidence one would have thought the role was already mine. I embodied the character and became just the right person for the role. When notified I had landed the role as Jeeper, I was too excited. What made it even better was this was my first SAG role, and for an actor, that's a big deal.

After wrapping up that opportunity, I continued my journey to obtain work and acting gigs. My journey led me to being the first and only African American to host a show on Fuse TV. The show was called IMX/Daily Download, and I was the host for three seasons. This opportunity was groundbreaking for me and truly took my desire to a different level. Even though I was honored to carry that badge of being the "first", it came with a price. Sometimes being the only one to do something is great, but sometimes it makes you stand alone. Plenty of times my manhood and pride in being African American were challenged. I constantly had to tiptoe around the concept of self-love and being non-threatening. How can you be less threatening when nothing about you is? That shit was hard to uphold! I was new to hosting, new to television, very young, and in a position that I'd never experienced before. I had millions of people watching me live every day, while executives blamed me for everything that went wrong. What a pressure-filled situation, right? And when the ratings started dropping, who do you think was to blame? It was clear to see what was happening. So, before they could get rid of me, I started auditioning for new roles or placement. I did not want their denial to be my adversity, but instead, my opportunity to achieve something greater. A couple of months later, just as I thought, my contract wasn't renewed, and it was on to the next opportunity doing voiceover work for two video games, "Def Jam Fight for NY" in 2004 and "The Warriors" in 2005.

As blessed as I was already, I could have never imagined the amount of blessings God was going to bless me with. I went from auditioning and praying for work to getting booked! My determination was bigger than the red carpets and fame many see when they come to Hollywood. I love acting and bringing characters to life. For those of us who do what we love, the adversity provides character and the struggle brings opportunity, but we have to remain commitment. I've had many reasons to quit and go back home to live a mundane 9-to-5 lifestyle; however, I trusted my gift and my ability to produce great characters and films.

However, when I landed my role in the movie "The Brave One" with actress Jodie Foster, it was truly game time. This opportunity and many auditions, while building working relationships, opened the door for many more movies and television appearances:

Movies:
Thank You for Your Service (2017)
Sweet Lorraine (2016)
Diamond Ruff (2015)
The Genesis of Lincoln (2014)
Captured Hearts (2013)
Dreams I & II (2013)
Changing the Game (2012)
Dysfunctional Friends (2012)
After Hours: The Movie (2011)
Code Blue (2010)
April's Fools (2010) - Tamil
Notorious (2009) - Damion
I Think I Love My Wife (2007)

Television:
Secrets (2017)
Bad Dad Rehab (2017)
Atlanta (2016)
Black Dynamite (2014)
Parenthood (2011-2013)
NYC 22 (2012)
The Closer (2010-2011)
Let's Talk About Pep ~ Episode #1.3 (2010)
Miracle's Boys (2005)
Jonny Zero (2005)
The Jury (2004)

One thing about being in Hollywood is you have to have knowledge of one's self to solidify your identity. As an African-American man, I have managed to be true to myself at all costs. Compromising myself for fame is not who I am nor is it how I was raised to be. Don't get me wrong, I love acting and being in front of the camera, but never at the price of losing who I am. On the flip side, I work hard to breathe life into every character I portray. I study who the character is, what they need from me, and how I can channel who I am to blend the pieces together. Now, remaining true to yourself may stop you from landing some roles, but never jeopardize your integrity and name for an industry that probably won't remember your name anyway. This is the true essence of surviving and being resilient in Hollywood.

Hollywood is no different than any other industry in this world. It's like a machine that never stops working. It has its own heartbeat and vision. That's how many people get bruised and broken within this world. They make the mistake of thinking they are the next big thing needed, not realizing that no one is bigger than the project. You simply add to the machine, but you will never control it. The goal is learning how to live within the premise of their story or taking control by creating your own lane that is recognized by the machine operators. Either way, your survival depends on you!

Having almost twenty years in the business, if you are looking to make that jump into acting or film, I would highly recommend you do these three things:

1. Make sure you take classes from people who are highly seasoned in the industry. Veterans in this business have a lot of pull and opportunities that can help hone your skills, while preparing you for an opportunity. I have my own acting school called "Act Like You Know", where I offer acting workshops and private coaching for beginners

who need that personal touch or advanced actors who need help preparing for a role or audition.

2. Study the industry, appreciate the history, understand the growth, and know the key players. If you are a writer, you should know who the head writers are, and the same with actors. You should never embark on a journey without first knowing who the players are and their contributions. We are all standing on the shoulders of others.

3. Stay dedicated. As I stated before, there will be more no's than yes's, and there will be times when you want to quit. But, if you take the no's and learn from them, your yes will be right around the corner. Everything in Hollywood is changing, and what use to be is now history. The good thing about this is that there are a lot of platforms available for you to share your gift and a lot of individuals who are waiting to help you elevate. But, you have to pay your dues and own your place in the room. Don't quit!

Adversity is a part of life! The key to surviving adversities is in how you handle them. How important is this journey to you? What is your breaking point? Why are you doing this? While going through this journey, I made sure I was clear on these questions and had solid answers for each. As you've read, I have been challenged and denied, but in that, no one can ever say I quit! I am living my dream and enjoying the ride along the way. Make sure you do anything in life for passion, because if it's for anything other than that, you will become vulnerable to being used, abused, mistreated, and pimped out. In this business, my mantra for self is, "Keep your dignity while pursuing your destiny." Hollywood is not for the faint of heart, but you can survive.

"My supreme motivation is to cultivate Actors, whether working or aspiring. That surplus of talent that is inside of you, I want to bring out and let it lead you to more roles and opportunities. Once you totally invest in your career & yourself, you will see a clearer path to success. As an Actor's Concierge, I will lend my extensive knowledge & experience to guide you to proper representation, precise audition techniques, career development & character connectivity. I want you to win, and you can."

~ **Dennis L.A. White**

Summer Fitch

Summer Willow Fitch, affectionately known as "Summer Willow" is a fun-loving Mixologist and the entrepreneur behind SummerWillow.com. During her tenure, Summer-Willow has "served" in several capacities including Mixology Instructor and Bar Management Consultant. She discovered her passion for concocting original recipes in the early stages of her career; which has significantly stamped her brand. She has a distinct reputation for creating classic original recipes, making her clients feel welcomed and served with a high level of professionalism. Her career behind-the-bar afforded her countless years of armchair therapy experience and influenced her first published book titled, *Let Me Tell You Like I Told Myself*, a compilation of reflections/advice given to her customers on love and relationships. Her literary contributions have been featured in major trade magazines, blogs, and published books.

Summer Willow Fitch holds an MBA with an

Entrepreneurship focus from Eastern University and lends her talent to coaching entrepreneurs and goal seekers across industries. Summer Willow is a proud Co-Founder of the Black Women Give Foundation (BWG) which seeks to engage and inspire African American women and girls in philanthropy by collectively funding impactful grants for organizations within underrepresented communities of color.

Potholes in My Lawn

I consider myself someone who enjoys nature. I am constantly in awe of all that God has created. I adore animals, flowers, the ocean, and the sun; but particularly I have a deep admiration for parks and large masses of grass. There is something so surreal about sitting in wide-open and green spaces, lush with sprouting grass for me to walk barefoot in, or softly lie upon with a book. I was born and raised in Germantown Philadelphia, and I have the pleasure of enjoying the beautiful green spaces known as Fairmount Park; one of the largest urban green spaces in the country. I am a city girl through and through, but I am a nature girl to the core.

    I remember being a small child hiking in Valley Green with my father; just me holding his hand, our canteen full of water, enjoying the sights and sounds of nature. My mother who has an enchanted green thumb would always include me in the planting of seedlings and bulbs to beautify our garden.

    As I grew older and started exploring on my own, my hikes were replaced by rides in my first car, a 1989 Nissan Maxima and my affinity for lush parks morphed into an obsession with landscaping. I am not good at it – but I love to behold a well-manicured, lush, and vibrant stretch of grass. I could sit for hours and just get lost in the smell of it. Understandably, curb appeal always catches my eye. Symbolically, I wanted to be that beautiful home with curb appeal. I wanted folks to slow down as they passed by me or want to sit in and around my vast existence and take me all in; I wanted to be admired for my natural beauty, as well.

I want to talk about the appearance of things and the reality of things. I always appeared to have it together but very few people knew my truth. At an early age, my life was riddled with trauma, confusion, and pain. The deep and dark places were hidden from passersby. My eyes, the windows to my soul, seemed clear and conscious to onlookers, but the glass was stained with images that I wished I had never seen. My soul was a basement flooded with tears, yet; all these deficiencies were masked by my sincere smile that I casually flash to acquaintances and family just like a beautiful entryway; let's face it, nothing says welcome like a beautiful front door. The truth, however, was that behind that door were only two sturdy structures; in my proverbial home, the only structures intact were the roof and the furnace. I am smart and all heart.

I made the outside so approachable and welcoming – but if you got too close to my home, you would find yourself sinking knee deep in the potholes. I never tended to these matters and as they got worse, I added more chains and deadbolts to my door for fear of confrontation on my hazardous behaviors. I created a smoke screen so no one would see my pain and I neglected my inside while keeping the outside maintained. However, in the summer of my 33rd birthday, I realized I could no longer pay for damages that I caused others and myself due to neglect. I was emotionally bankrupt.

It took a very tumultuous time and extreme feelings of frustration otherwise known as, "Hitting rock bottom" for me to start thinking that I should seek counseling. I went and poured out my heart – hoping for the tools to begin healing. With the help of therapy, loving family, and friends, I excavated my soul and began to fill it with healthy, wealthy, and prosperous soil where beautiful things could grow. Three massive potholes got my immediate attention:

1. Self-Image
My self-image was compromised at a very young age due to sexual abuse, witnessing verbal and physical abuse and the unstable relationships of my parents. I felt horrible about myself and allowed the actions of others to make me feel worthless and disposable. I struggled heavily with this as a child and felt even more disconnected to rehabilitating this issue in my adult life. Inside I grew up feeling ugly and less than – yet I smiled. I was loved by my parents very sincerely and very openly but the things that I saw and felt scarred me. I kept so much inside that I began to feel dead and relegated to a life of shame and secrets. I needed to purge all of the images and perspectives of those that I allowed to influence my self-talk and self-esteem. In order to begin to see myself for the beautiful spirit that I was – I had to move differently.

At the age of 33, I decided after another failed relationship that I should seek therapy. At first, it was hard to commit to seeing a therapist due to the stigma in my community about airing your dirty laundry to strangers – but the truth was, the people in my circle could not help me. My self-perception was not pretty, polished, or put together, but after a few months, at least I began to see the real me.

My unbiased therapist uncovered shameful memories and feelings that I hid in order to function; she revealed the fact that I never truly grieved the pains of my childhood. This was one of the most difficult parts of my healing process. In order to have a healthy self-image, I had to expose my unhealthy self and process why she no longer served my life's purposes. Shedding tears and forgiving people was difficult but I did it. It was most difficult to forgive those who never said sorry – but I learned to take my power back and that meant I did not need anyone to fill those holes in my heart – those potholes were sufficiently filled in peace and solitude by me alone.

2. Belief in my highest self and my creativity

I have always been a creative child. I was singing full songs before I could speak full sentences. I play 3 instruments and I am self-taught. I was a professional singer for 24 years and currently a songwriter and producer. On the academic front, I wear my Blerd badge with honor. I won science, math, and writing contest all through school. I was a continuous honor roll student, Senior Class President of Germantown High School, Black Student Union President while attending West Chester University and won the race for homecoming queen of the West Chester University in 1998. I pledged Zeta Phi Beta Sorority, Inc. I started my own business SummerWillow.com in 2002 and earned an MBA with an entrepreneurship focus in 2007. I am a mixologist and so much more and I truly have a passion for all that I do. Sounds like I have it going on, right? Back to that green lush grass, I was talking about – yeah that next pothole I needed to fix was believing in myself.

When you doubt who you are, you become unsure of who you can be. I have always had awesome ideas and I executed them all while doubting every step. Prior to receiving therapy, making moves was not my challenge, it was my destructive self-talk. I would talk myself out of doing things before I even took the first step. I would write amazing business plans for myself and then decide – Nah. I would forego working on my own business to help others thrive and most destructively – I would downplay my ideas to others. It was truly an ineffective habit that led me to be stagnant because of fear. People would always compliment me and tell me they wanted my help with their business but I felt like their visions would be more successful than mine. So, I helped many people, free of charge, to live their dreams. Meanwhile, I was growing deeper in debt to self and it was time to pay up. I was not securing myself and my goals and I let people use my business ideas and savvy to grow their riches - but I was broke and broken.

3. Lack of Action

I think about the song "Potholes in my Lawn" by De La Soul and my experience hearing it for the first time. It was 1989 and I was 12 years old. I just loved the cadence and the beat and it pulled me in, but I totally missed the message. Now that I am older and I have gone through some things, I actually understand the message and how it applies to me. I do not write rhymes but I have written ideas on the scrolls of my soul and I was allowing the world to steal, and claim my identity yet do it no justice. This had to stop.

After therapy, I felt I had the tools I needed to help myself. I knew what I was looking at in the mirror and I knew what I needed to do to fix it. I wrote everything down.

I have papers from 1996 of business ideas and marketing campaigns for ideas I wanted to grow. My challenge was believing in myself and making those things happen. I was paralyzed by the fear of failure and it was laughable. I would run and jump for others while doing nothing for myself – I was failing the entire time. The fault there was that I was failing for nothing. I was not taking any risks and putting myself in any position to win. How could I possibly learn anything operating like that? How could I grow? I had to stop setting myself up for the win yet refusing to play the game just because I was afraid of losing.

  The first step I took was to send out a survey to just about everyone I knew asking two very simple questions. "Give me two words you would use to describe me" and "How have I influenced your life, if at all"? The response was overwhelming. First of all – everyone responded. That showed me that my circle of influence was great and that I had a support system when all the while feeling lonely. Secondly, there was a very large portion of responses from people saying that I encouraged them to get their education. This shocked me because I took my education for granted and I did not think that I used my degree wisely – meaning I was not getting rich, but I was not getting rich or building wealth because I was not pushing and focused on doing so. Finally, I read that a lot of responses stating that I was a great entrepreneur and they were proud of my business offerings. These people found me to be a nice person and genuine soul.

  After I received the survey responses I switched gears quickly. I began to very purposefully build my brand, my product and service offerings, and my customer base. I stopped judging myself and putting myself into a box and I celebrated my brand. I am a mixologist. I wrote a book. I am a book editor. I am business savvy. I can create a brand. I can do anything that I want to do.

However, no one can want it more than me. I am so proud to say that SummerWillow.com has transformed; I am now SummerWillow.com Lifestyle: Mind, Body, and Spirits and I cater to all of my passions because I say so. I love myself and I love what I do. I wanted to fix the potholes in my lawn. I wanted to fill the voids in my life. I understood that I have a lot of work to do and I continue to improve. 7 years later I am exactly where I need to be. No one can tell me that I am too old or young to do what I am destined to do and be. I filled those potholes and now there is grass growing I am consistently repairing my house so that the inside and the outside are both cared for and I am healthy, wealthy, and prosperous. Cheers.

Anissa Zabriskie

(In picture: Susie Carder, Anissa Zabriskie, Lisa Nichols)

    Anissa Zabriskie, MBA, PHR, SHRM-CP is a global Human Resource professional with over 20 years of human resources and organizational development experience. Anissa's expertise includes talent management, organizational development, training and development, and leadership and management coaching.

    Anissa is passionate about helping businesses make the most of their resources and talent. In addition to her accomplishments in HR/OD, Anissa is a volunteer leader for the Society for Human Resource Management (SHRM) where she donates time on the political advocacy committee. Anissa has organized one-on-one coaching, group workshops, and educational seminars at colleges and universities to empower students to find jobs upon graduating.

As a trained speaker and DDI (Development Dimensions International, Inc.) licensed facilitator, Anissa has presented in boardrooms across the globe including Singapore, Taiwan and South Korea. Anissa holds a Bachelor of Science and a Master's degree in Business Administration.

An avid pet lover, Anissa lives in the Boston area with her husband, two cats and dog. You can reach Anissa at Anissaz.iss@gmail.com

The Wounds of Time Can Be Healed

Close your eyes and think back to a time when you were growing up and there was a kid on your block that you befriended. The two of you played games, perhaps you went to the neighborhood candy store, rode bikes to the park, or chased the ice cream truck down the street on hot summer days. Then one day, that childhood friend moves away. Of course, both of you vow to stay in touch by writing emails, calling, or even make plans to visit one another. In many cases, due to the dynamic we refer to as life, that just does not happen and you lose touch forever.

During our lifetime, there are numerous experiences everyone will have involving other people. Sometimes those experiences are wonderful. A person enters our lives and we learn something and we grow emotionally or spiritually. We learn to love better, communicate better, dress better, and ultimately, we feel better. And then, that person is gone.

Oh… you can open your eyes now if you haven't already…

I am going to share how my life connections helped me grow spiritually and physically and the purpose of me sharing is that you are inspired, motivated, and determined to see every interaction as a growth connection in your own life.

BRUISED

I am one of five children, born to a draftsman and a schoolteacher in Gary, Indiana in 1970. I would never get to know my birth parents. Several months after I was born, I was given up for adoption to an orphanage in Chicago. I moved around to different foster homes until I was finally adopted at 10 months old. I grew up in a strict household on Chicago's Southside. Things went well except for the fact that from the age of 5 to the age of 14 a family friend sexually abused me.

At the time, I didn't realize that an adult was not supposed to touch a child this way. No one in my home ever discussed what to do if these things happened. I told my mother one day when she and I were walking around in our backyard. The only reason I mentioned it was because I'd learned from my physical education classes that I could become pregnant. Telling my mom was so difficult, especially when I could tell how hurt she was inside. It was obvious every time she looked at me she was reminded of the trauma I had suffered.

Unfortunately, the scars of abuse were damaging. As a result, I contemplated suicide many times as a teen and struggled emotionally through high school. It was not until I was an adult that I realized suicide would be a permanent solution to a temporary problem. Finally, in 1990, my parents could no longer handle my emotional issues and forced me to leave home. At the age of 20, I had nowhere to go and only a used 1979 Dodge Aspen and a part-time job at a local restaurant to survive on.

I was in college at the time and continued my studies at Chicago State University as I worked several jobs to pay bills and maintain my studio apartment. Many asked me why I didn't quit school and just work full-time but despite my issues, I was on a mission to be the best I could be. While in college, I joined Army ROTC (Reserve Officers Training Corps)—one of the most demanding and successful leadership programs in the country. The U.S. Army Cadet Command selects, educates, trains, and commissions college students to be officers and leaders of character in the Total Army; instills the values of citizenship, national and community service, personal responsibility, and a sense of accomplishment in high school students. Army ROTC saved my life by providing me structure and discipline and later in 1994, it guided me to a degree in Business Administration. Many of the friends I made while in ROTC, I still stay in touch with today.

BROKEN

In 2017 the average person changes jobs twelve times over the course of a career, according to the Bureau of Labor Statistics. There's a pretty good chance at least one job change won't be by choice.

In August 2008, like many Americans, I found myself a victim of the recession. I still remember the meeting I had at four P.M. on a Monday afternoon with my manager in the HR director's office. I was now married and this was one year after I had relocated my husband, Richard, and our two cats from our affordable home in Phoenix, Arizona to the more expensive Stewartsville, New Jersey for a major biotech company. Richard had left his secure job of 20 years to help me pursue my dreams of being a Human Resource executive. We were obligated for mortgages on both the Phoenix home and New Jersey residency, and the bills were mounting. I felt like such a failure. How was I going to pay two mortgages? How was I going to keep the utilities on? Panic set in.

I found this new job almost immediately but I fell into a deep depression once I landed it. For over 2 years I beat myself up mentally. To hold on to my sanity, I read a chapter a day from the Bible. It may not seem like much, but the thirty minutes, or so, that I spent reading, helped to clear my mind and cleanse my soul. I joined the local YMCA to stay active and have a strong sense of community. These life-altering steps helped me to heal my bruises and emotional scars and push forward. Most importantly, I realized that the job I was desperately trying to hang on to was one of the many life connections that I had made. I had added value to that company for a particular time, after which, it was time for me to move on and share my talents and expertise elsewhere.

BLESSED

As I was writing this chapter, I sat in the leather chair in my office at work and gazed out of the sliding glass windows and thought, *I am blessed!* I have a wonderful career that permits me to coach and counsel scientists and engineers who invent some of the most amazing innovations of our era.

I spent 20 years wondering who my biological parents were but in early 2000, I researched and determined my parents were no longer alive. My mother died of breast cancer and my father died of natural causes. I am dedicated now to finding out what has become of my other four siblings. The search will continue.

With prayer and counseling, I have been able to put the abuse and emotional trauma behind me. I came to realize that I couldn't be a failure to those who sacrificed before me. I couldn't fail the legacy of my biological parents who raised four children in Gary, Indiana and had to make a life changing decision to put me up for adoption, in hopes that I would have a richer life. I must triumph for my birth mother who carried me for nine months, knowing that she may not be able to keep and raise me. When I am still and quiet, I can feel her pain and I decided that I have to be a success as a reward for her sacrifice.

I am determined to be a success for my adopted parents who took a child into their home to love and care for. Because my loving husband, who sacrificed his own career, home, and stability, that I might be able to purse my dreams—I have to be a success. For all the sisters and brothers in the world who have been adopted, abused or lost everything—I hope these words will empower you to keep going on in life and NEVER GIVE UP.

Kenneth Nelson

Kenneth Nelson is native of Southern California, born in Los Angeles, raised in San Bernardino. Graduate of Lincoln University with a BA in Liberal Arts Education and MS in Exercise Science. He has been in the Fitness Profession for 24+ years. His journey started as a trainer at Holiday Spa in Glendora California, which was the original Bally Total Fitness. He has previously held the position of Fitness Director and Manager for Bally Total Fitness, Fitness 19, La Fitness, and Gold Gym. Currently, he is the COO of his own Fitness/Wellness Company, Phit Club and the CEO/ Owner of FitZonFit. Phit Club is the annex for Trainers in Philadelphia to have a place to train clients. In addition to personal training, Kenneth designs personalized fitness and nutritional programs that fit each individual needs based on where they want to be, where they are and where they were.

Kenneth is known in the Fitness World as Dr. Fitness because of his approach to Fitness. "I am a physician when it comes to my clients and anyone that has fitness questions. My philosophy is Fitness is internal, it starts from the inside. My motto is "Stay Strong Get Stronger", he says.

Against All Odds...
A Story of Struggle and Beating the Odds

It has been said that life is a gamble and every day you wake up you have to deal with the hand you are dealt. Sometimes you win, sometimes you lose, and sometimes you fold, but at the end of the day, you pray to be granted the opportunity to play a new hand and eventually beat the odds. As a kid, I had a decent childhood. I am the middle child of 9 siblings, had a nice home, dogs, a yard to play in and toys; all the basics a child could ever want or need. The most important thing I always had was my family. We were, and continue to be tight as a knot in a shoestring, and at times we are inseparable. My father was an officer and retired veteran, and my mother was a real estate agent and housewife. I thought we had it all, and we did; however, in the blink of an eye, we lost it all.

It was the summer leading into my freshman year in high school; after the last two years of moving from home to home, we finally got settled with some family friends. My parents had been gone for a year now. Not deceased, but in a rehab facility in Santa Monica. No one knew but us and our surrogate family, Mama Dee, and George. They took us in. At the time, my oldest sister Lisa was in Anaheim, my second oldest sister, Jivonne, had gone to the military, my third oldest, DeShante, went back to Los Angeles to live with her biological father and that left me, my fourth oldest sister, Kennetta (my twin for a day), 3 younger brothers, (Johnie, Stephan and Timothy) and younger sister Tammy. All of us sleeping on the living room floor of Mama Dee's three bedroom house that was inhabited by her family, three daughters, and their boyfriends. Calling us sardines was an understatement. As the man of the family, my only job was to make sure that we stayed together.

My parents left us in order to get their lives back in order and I didn't understand until I was 16. For years no one knew that my parents were gone and every day I would return to the place we called home hoping that I would walk in and see them. After a while, I stopped hoping. As my siblings struggled to deal, focus on school, and make friends, I assumed the role of big brother and father. I worked to make sure we had everything we needed and I worked harder to make sure we never had to depend on anyone ever again. We tried to live normal lives; all of us were playing sports with the exception of my younger brother who was an artistic and computer genius. For the most part, we were together and for the most part, happy. Then, our secret got out. Trying to hide our parent's absence was not as easy as I thought it would be. In fact, it got harder and harder as I grew older. Being a 16-year-old young man with work, athletics, and a girlfriend, made playing daddy to four siblings an exhausting challenge, but I actually managed it all until child services got involved. If it wasn't for my grandmother we would have never stood a chance at staying together.

My trajectory into a career in fitness was an easy decision. It all started with my passion for sports and my parents' experimentation with drugs; don't knock them because it's not an uncommon phenomenon. Between my disdain for cigarette smoke and my hatred for what drugs did to my family, fitness was my only career path and choice next to teaching health. I was an athlete, good at every sport, but baseball was my strong point. Some would say that basketball was my strong point, but the way my height was set up I did not really think the NBA would have been an option. I had an opportunity to have a successful baseball career but I chose family first. I wish I knew then what I know now. I would probably be playing pro baseball, or maybe not, but I was going in the right direction thanks to God and a significant support system. I always heard that you can be anything you want if you just put your mind to it. Well, my mind said, "WTF! Why is this happening to me?"

Freshman Year, San Bernardino High School the place where my career began. My mentors have always been my P. E. teachers and coaches because as an athlete I figured they would understand me more. I was right to an extent but they saw my physical talent and knew nothing about my emotional torment. Not that it was any fault of theirs but because I held it in, there was no way I was going to let anyone know my family situation. So I hid my emotions, which is probably the reason I function the way I do at times. My coaches and teachers only knew what they saw and they helped as much as they could. This is where my passion for fitness took flight. I thought for the longest time that my physical stature was going to limit my ability to become a pro athlete, but that isn't the only thing needed. I needed to also develop some mental and emotional toughness as well. These are the three components of fitness; but back to my story. Freshman year was a struggle and hiding my abandonment issues was an even bigger struggle; it was a gamble that I was willing to take in order to beat the odds against us.

We walked five plus miles to school every morning, had to leave by 5 am in order to make it to class on time at 7:15am. Now I know why I get up so early. Sometimes we had the luxury of the bus if I made enough hustle money, but most of the time we walked. Walking in Cali wasn't bad; the weather was nice 80 percent of the time. We got caught in some rain every now and then but it was rare. We used our old address in order for us to remain in the district, but the sacrifice associated to that was our daily commuting adventure. My siblings went to Arrowview Middle School, my old stomping grounds where I adopted the idea of becoming a gym teacher. I had two of the best, Coach Leiritz and Coach Eatinger. They didn't really know about our struggles, which began my final year at Arrowview, yet, they always made sure we got home after games and didn't mind buying a burger or two. The struggle was real. I kept my composure and my pride at the same time. While our day to day going through the motions continued, we had to maintain our silence. I worked a paper route, ran errands, and worked landscaping every chance I got. I dabbled in some minor activities when things got real tight. But all in all, I kept working. My sister had a prom coming and I wanted to make sure she went while also making certain we had food to eat. Through it all, I still had time for basketball, baseball and volunteered as a coach at Arrowview, where I had the opportunity to coach both of my brothers and my younger sister. I never asked why any of this was happening to a 16-year-old. Why was I being forced to be an adult before my time? Then one day I broke down. All my emotions came out at one time.

Sophomore and junior year flew by. We learned how to just move on and keep moving. My parents returned towards the end of my junior year. We pretended like nothing happened because at the end of the day what can you do. But our story came out. It was only a matter of time before someone figured out that a 16-year-old boy was taking care of five siblings. We only went to the doctor if we were hurt. We had no need for the dentist because we could not afford candy. My break down was inevitable. I was tired of not having a life. I met a young lady, Cindy. She was absolutely the woman I knew was for me. Young love is amazing because you know nothing but you think you know everything. She was the best; we never had any issues but she made me put my guard down. As soon as I lowered my guard I started to get hit with punches and my break down began. Our secret became public shortly after.

Now that my parents were back, my younger siblings moved back with them. I chose to stay with my grandmother. For once in my teenage life, I had a stable place. My relationship grew, and I was truly a man. This turn of events in my life made me such an emotional wreck and I had to speak to someone. I decided to tell my story in an essay that my Principal read. Principal Karen Craig, who was like a mother to me, read what has been happening to us for the past 2 ½ years. In her tears, she said, "I'm sorry that this happened to you". Stuff like this doesn't happen to

Scholar-Athletes. She shared my story with my counselor. I was called into the counselors' office in February of '94. Ms. Stenson and Ms. Hayes just hugged me. That was the first time I cried in 4 years. The last time I cried was the day my parents went to rehab and my mother and father asked me to make sure we stayed together. My counselors couldn't believe that we had this secret for so long. They never would have thought because of the way we carried ourselves and how we would behave every day for those past 2 ½ years. My parents didn't technically leave us. They left us in good hands for the time being; at least that's what I told myself for years. I knew what it meant to be completely abandoned and that wasn't what happened to us. But hey you say tomato, I say to-mah-to. My fear of separation from my siblings became a story of courage, determination, and perseverance.

I was advised by Ms. Craig and Ms. Stenson to tell my story. Overnight I became a celebrity, well a small 10 minute news report and paper segment celebrity. My story was out and I never imagined or realized the support and help that I was going to receive. Channel 6 news aired my story and they actually followed us as we went on a day that was normal for us, but sad for anyone else that knew us. We relived the 5-mile walks we used to make to school every day. Even the reporters were just in disbelief. It was disbelief because it was not just me, but was all of us. I held us down and kept it very normal. In 1994, I became a Night of the Beautillion Scholarship recipient and a "Beat the Odds" scholarship recipient. Beat the Odds is a scholarship sponsored by Channel 6 News. During this time my sister Kennetta was a senior in route to graduate with honors. I was a junior playing varsity baseball. My siblings were back with my parents and still doing well in school. We were still struggling but my parents were clean. I was living with my grandmother until I graduated. I was introduced to my mentor Dr. Ernest C Levister, who got me into college at his Alma Mater and now my Alma Mater Lincoln University. From the time I met those odds, to the time I beat the odds, I had a heavy weight on my shoulders. The day of the Beat the Odds Awards ceremony that weight was lifted.

It was a bright April day, the last baseball game of the season. I was a second string outfielder hoping to get in the game. My parents came to the game. They had never been to any of my high school baseball games; not one. Coach knew about the ceremony so he already had planned to get me in the game. When my parents came he made it official. I came around the fence hugged my mom and told her that everything was going to be ok. I hugged and high fived my dad and told him that I understood everything and I no longer need to know why. Then I took my normal spot on the bench and cheered my teammates on. It was the bottom of the seventh inning and I had to go get ready for the awards banquet. As I got ready to leave coach said, "Nelson go to right field". At that moment I knew that everything was going to really be ok. The score was 4 -3 with two outs. Next thing you hear is the ping of a bat and a fly ball came my way. Behind me was Ms. Craig telling me we have to go because I'm going be late. In Front of me was my first fly ball in a Varsity baseball game. In the bleachers was my parents and girlfriend cheering as I camped under the ball. At home was my grandmother who saved our lives. In the parking lot waiting were my siblings coming to celebrate my recognition. At first and third base were guys from the other team running to score. It seemed like that ball hung in the air for an eternity. When that ball was hit, the last 4 years of my life flashed before my eyes and I couldn't breathe. I caught the ball, the game was over, I did a full hurdle over the right-field fence, grabbed my suit from Ms. Craig and ran into the locker room to change for the Beat the Odds Award Ceremony. I left everything on the field that day. I left all of the odds that were against me on the field that day. That evening I received my award from Victoria Rowell and Jon Voight. Dr. Levister, Ms. Stenson, Ms. Craig, my grandmother, and most importantly my siblings were there in the audience. My parents were not there but they saw me play and that was enough for me. As I accepted my award I took a deep breath and exhaled.

Today, I am a Fitness Entrepreneur, a father of two beautiful girls (Michelle & Londyn), an educator, a coach, and still a brother to my now grown and successful siblings. I didn't beat the odds; we beat the odds, together! That 2 ½ years of my life really shaped the man that I am now. Yet, it was God and determination that got us through that rough time, and family that got me to where I am now. Every day I am teaching people how to beat the odds. When you think you cannot do it, you can. Results are in your grasp you just have to reach for them. Be disciplined and determined and you will reach your goals. Whether they are fitness, economic, educational, relationship, employment, or whatever; reach out, take charge and embrace your fears. Better yet, take charge without fear. You never know when you are going to "Beat the Odds". Remember that life is short but FAMILY IS FOREVER. You can overcome any obstacle in front of you and just believe that you can overcome.

Roberta A. Albany

After being diagnosed with Breast Cancer in December 2013 while training for her first half marathon and served as a Running Coordinator for a Philadelphia Running Group. Roberta wanted to know more about her type of Breast Cancer (Estrogen Positive) which she became a very active and trained advocate for herself and others.

Roberta's advocacy and membership began with Living Beyond Breast Cancer as a Young Women's Advocate, the American Cancer Society as a Reach for Recovery Volunteer, Volunteer for the Pennsylvania Breast Cancer Coalition, the National Coalition for Cancer Survivorship and the National Breast Cancer Coalition where Roberta graduated from their Project Lead Institute in July 2017. These organizations afforded Roberta the opportunity to become more involved in her community at large, especially medical personnel and government officials. Roberta is a retired government employee and currently enjoys traveling, spending time with family and friends.

Roberta has a son Stephen who resides in Virginia with his wife (Cheryl) who are very successful in their careers. Roberta lives in Pennsylvania.

Contact Info:
Email address is roberta.albany@outlook.com
Instagram: @roberta.albany
Twitter:@raalbany
Facebook: Roberta A Albany

My "Why" After Breast Cancer

I figure what more could life throw at me after being a victim of child abuse and then surviving domestic abuse. Being sexual assaulted when I was 36 years old and having to overcome the trauma of that experience, only to hear my physician tell me at 44, "You Have Breast Cancer". Hearing this made me truly numb because I've been getting mammograms since I was thirty, due to having a partial hysterectomy. After having this procedure they told me that I would be more prone to developing breast cancer, but during that time I never really paid any attention to that information because I was going through a divorce and trying to build a "new me".

In April 2013, I had my annual mammogram and was told that everything was normal, and so I moved forward with purchasing a new home and car. Remembering what the doctors had told me after my partial hysterectomy, I looked at this "normal" as a clean bill of health. I like to make sure that my health is in order before I make big purchases and have some hiccups to get in the way. So after hearing that news, I went back to enjoying life and participating in various activities in Philadelphia. I was so elated that I even became the running coordinator for a group of runners in Philadelphia, while training for my first half-marathon. While going through the vigorous training, I kept having pain in my left breast. Initially, I figured it was because I was lifting weights, but the pain was persistent. After a while, I decided to do a breast exam to see if I felt anything or if anything felt weird. So I lay down on my living room floor and I began examining and feeling for something, anything to where as I can self-diagnosis myself and finally put this pain to rest. As I was feeling around, I discovered a lump on the left side that was closer to my arm pit. Immediately I thought, "Here we go again"! Because my breast were considered fibrocystic, there were times when I felt a lump and go get it tested, and told that it wasn't anything to worry about. Could this be any different? Who knows, but the next day, I called my gynecologist to tell her about my discovery and made an appointment. My appointment was scheduled for November 2013, and she indicated that she wanted me to get a mammogram along with an ultrasound. I told myself that there was nothing wrong and that it'll be okay. I tried not to worry! After surviving child and domestic abuse and sexual assault, God wouldn't let anything else bad happen to me, right! I held onto that, until it was the day of my appointment and the nurse came into the waiting area and said, "Ms. Albany, we need to talk to you about seeing a breast surgeon as soon as possible" and ever so kindly handed me materials regarding breast health resources. The nurse made it very clear to me that my appointment with the breast surgeon will be fast track and at that point, my heart sank.

  I scheduled the appointment with the breast surgeon for December 17, 2013, but this time around my aunt went with me. During this visit, the surgeon did a fine needle aspiration (FNA) biopsy of the lump that was directly under my armpit. A fine needle aspiration biopsy is where the doctor uses a very thin, hollow needle attached to a syringe to withdraw (aspirate) a small amount of tissue or fluid from a suspicious area. The biopsy sample is then checked to see if there are cancer cells in it. After the biopsy, they told me that the sample would be going to lab and that I will be hearing something from them in a few days. Not worried, I went on life once again, but then on December 19, 2013 while enjoying my job's Christmas luncheon I received the call that would change my life. The surgeon called! He asked if I was alone and I said yes, there was a moment of silence and then without any sign of caution he proceeded to tell me, "I hate to do this to you but the results from the needle aspiration came back and unfortunately *You Have Breast Cancer*".

    Initially, I was devastated. He continued to tell me what I needed to do and we hung up the telephone. I went back to the luncheon trying to maintain my composure and pretend that I did not hear what I just heard. I was hoping that nobody saw my facial expression or sense of disbelief, but a particular coworker realized something wasn't quite right with me. After the luncheon we ended up in the same room together, but alone, and without thought or fear of judgement, I burst out crying. I shared with her what the breast surgeon told me that I have breast cancer and she just held me and told me to just to let it out. And trust you and me that is all I could do. There wasn't a tear left within me after that. After I got myself together, all I wanted to do was go home and be with my family.

    I remember driving on highway 422, I had called my son to tell him what I've learned and instead of an immediate response, there was silence on his end. Talking about it again, made me get emotional but I knew driving and crying was not the smartest thing to do because I had to pay attention to the traffic. Finally, my son responded and I could hear his voice breaking up and eventually he asked me, "what are we going to do about this situation" and I was able to inform him that, "I have several appointments lined up to get this crap out of my body!" After we hung up, the next call I made was to my aunt and I told her too but now I am crying. It was dark outside, my eyes were full of tears, and I am just frustrated that once again, I am the recipient of something. Why Me?? My aunt was upset that I was driving in the dark under such bad condition and instead of consoling; her focus went to making sure I made it home safely.

After making it home, and finally getting to sit and digest what I really heard that surgeon say, I got ANGRY as HELL! I had so many questions. Like, how in the hell did this happened when they told me that my mammogram was normal back in April 2013, only to be diagnosed in December 2013! I was trying to figure out how do I, Roberta A Albany, have breast cancer when I did everything that the doctors told me to do with regards to exercising, eat healthy, maintain a healthy weight, blah, blah, blah. Was there anything else I could have done to prevent it? Was it heredity? Where did it come from? So many questions, with no answers!

Towards the end of December 2013 going into January 2014, there was nothing but tests after tests. Thank God, the many test finally enabled someone to answer my DAMN questions about why I have breast cancer! Apparently, because my breasts are so dense there was a possibility that the mammogram machines would not detect cancer. You would think that someone would have given me a heads-up about this. So even though I had mammograms after mammograms, it was the ultrasound that detected the cancer in my breast. Go Figure!! Once all of the tests were done, including genetic testing, I was officially diagnosed with Stage IIB, Estrogen Positive, Grade 3, Invasive Ductal Carcinoma. Still trying to understand these diagnoses, the physicians explained to me that they couldn't save my left breast because there were way too many tumors. So on February 26, 2014, I had a radical mastectomy, at which point, they removed all seventeen of my lymph nodes, but only two came back positive for cancer. Several days later, I was released from the hospital. My God, it took me several weeks before I was finally able to look at myself in the mirror once the nurse removed all of the dressings and bandages from the surgery. When I finally got the heart to look at the "new me", I stood there crying like a baby because there was a long scar going across the left side where MY BREAST once lived. I turned to look at my other breast and that was just as healthy - talk about being lopsided! As I stared at this craziness and then looked up to look into my own eyes, I became angry once again that this happened to me. Like, WHY ME? But before I could go into my questions again, I got myself together because I knew that the next part of my journey needed my faith and strength if I wanted to survive.

The journey to chemotherapy wasn't as bad for me and I have to say that it was because I had an awesome support system, especially since my aunt and girlfriend became the entertainment duo for the nurses and patients. Those conversations were something else!! On the other hand, radiation sucked! Five weeks for 15 to 20 minutes everyday being burned to a crisp wasn't entertaining at all, with or without my aunt or girlfriend. However, I have to thank God for the American Cancer Society (Hope Lodge) because they gave me a home away from home so that I could relax and enjoy the beautiful scenery. Do absolutely nothing while my caregivers truly took care of me which meant no cooking or cleaning. Just relaxation and enjoy the other survivors and making lifelong friendships.

In addition, I was able to stay along with my caregivers while I was receiving my radiation treatments. During this part of the journey, I became very depressed, lost faith, and alcohol became my very close friend. To help keep some kind of normalcy during this time, I was still participating with my Philadelphia running group, but they were unaware of what I was going through. I hid this from them because I didn't want anyone to feel sorry for me and I wasn't quite ready to share my trials and tribulations. They found out in February 2016, during me speaking at an event that one of my beautiful friends asked me to share my story. It was then that I revealed to the world what I've been dealing with behind closed doors with regards to the cancer, radiation, depression, losing my faith, alcohol, and questioning God. Yes I DID, questioned GOD – WHY! Again, how could someone like me and after all I've already been through be chosen to go through more? During that speech I revealed how I'd lost friends, well whom I thought were my friends, after being diagnosed. I talked about how along the way I would in return gain life savers and the real beautiful friends, one in particular who would have stayed by my side since the initial diagnosis. I tell people that she's my, "ride to die bestie for life". Once I finished speaking another beautiful friend got up to speak and I remember her saying that she was going to speak on something else but after hearing my speech and witnessing herself how I was showing up for our meetups, she revealed to us what she had struggled with as a child and adult. All I could say was WOW! In that moment, all I could think about was how it's so important that we love on one another and be kind to one another because you really never know what someone is going or have gone through in their lives.

After that event, I realized that I needed to get myself out of this funk that I was in. I did so by getting a therapist and attending various support groups in person and online. With the help of my therapist and support groups I did the work that was needed to get to what most survivors like to call it 'new normal'. Another one of my beautiful friends introduce me to someone who was a survivor and she became my mentor and very close friend. We would talk on the telephone for hours since the both of us had sleeping problems. We confided in one another about our struggles with breast cancer and the constant medical issues we had to deal with, along with family and relationship issues. During our conversations I remember her specifically asking me about what I did for a living and it was then we realized that we were both state employees and had very stressful and demanding jobs. In that moment, she offered me the best advice ever. She told me to, "remove as much stress from my life and more importantly remove myself from toxic situations that didn't have my best interest at heart". Didn't I say, "the best advice ever"! As time went on she said to me that once I completed the work that I needed to do for myself, she wanted me to become more involved with various breast cancer organizations. I agreed and after completing all of my treatments and countless surgeries in

September 2014, I went to my first breast cancer conference called Living Beyond Breast Cancer Fall Conference which was held at the Loews Hotel in Philadelphia, PA. I knew my mentor wasn't going to be there, but she told me to look for one particular survivor that lives in Pennsylvania so I wouldn't feel so alone. In the process of me looking for the survivor from Pennsylvania who has a beautiful and bubbly personality that I love; I was greeted by another beautiful survivor from Atlanta who's personality was just as big as her pretty smile. We met because while walking I looked lost and she introduced herself as well as I did and we began talking until the other survivor showed up. At this conference I learned so much about breast cancer and the various sub types of breast cancer. I saw so many young and older women who understood what I've been going through and still was going through. I was not alone and if are going through as well, you are not alone either. As time went on I had learned that there were problems-women who look like me but were dying at a higher rate while other women were surviving! Why the disparity? Here is where my advocacy became my life's passion. In September 2015, I applied and was accepted to be a Young Women's Advocate for Living Beyond Breast Cancer. *Living Beyond Breast Cancer's Young Advocate Program* provides the tools and training to help young women use their personal breast cancer experience to make a difference in their communities by raising awareness, further their understanding of the disease and advocate for others. The training was held in Denver, Colorado and here is where I met another beautiful survivor who was my roommate and a great match.

As my advocacy grew, I became more involved with several other organizations that deal with all cancers like:

National Cancer Coalition for Survivorship, American Cancer Society, Living Beyond Breast Cancer, and the National Breast Cancer Coalition. This one sparked my interest because of the science/biology of breast cancer. Each of these organizations has afforded me different opportunities to be a part of the solution and bridge the disparity gap that I learned about previously. So much so, that I am now a patient advocate and member of the cancer committees at Abington Jefferson Health where I received my treatment and a member and co-chair of Shades of Brown Foundation nonprofit organization – Philadelphia Chapter.

Remember how I questioned God about "WHY ME?", I finally received my answer. Sometimes in life, we go through trials, tribulations, and turmoil, but did you know that those testimonies are meant to be shared. God puts you through, sees you through so that you can be of service and pass on the wisdom and know how that saved you. Even when I lacked faith, he showed me the way through and still helping me through as I have now been 4 years of no evidence of disease. But would I be celebrating this milestone if I would have kept my story silent? There is salvation in your story, and there is grace in your service, and this is why I am still standing. This is my WHY? I went from living before to cancer to living in abundance afterwards, and for that I am grateful.

So now, My Why" is clear, "Being of service to those whom are less fortunate than myself, educating the community about the importance of breast cancer and informing the community about the various organizations that's available to those persons who may need it".

Be your own ADVOCATE and more importantly know your body LADIES and GENTLEMEN.

Latisha Stephens

Latisha Stephens is a Goal Strategist, Personal Life Coach, Mompreneur and Real Estate Broker that specializes in property management. She has helped hundreds of people reduce anxiety, manage risk, and improve quality of life by assisting them with identifying their vision, developing S.M.A.R.T. and meaningful goals and creating action plans with follow up support; analyzing the effectiveness of the plan and revising the goals and interventions, as needed.

Her goals in life are simple-to finish raising her four healthy, productive children, enjoy her awesome husband, effectively and successfully maintain her personal businesses, help as many people as possible become their own risk managers and be a positive change agent through facilitation of self-improvement strategies, goal identification and awareness. Graduate of Albany State University and

Strayer University and proud member of Delta Sigma Theta Sorority, Incorporated, Latisha has one mantra she lives by, "WRITE | TAKE ACTION | WIN."

Join Latisha's mailing list at www.latishastephens.com for news about her coaching business, new books and upcoming appearances in her area. Email questions to hello@latishastephens.com. Follow her on Facebook at Facebook.com/CoachLatisha and on Instagram @CoachLatisha.

Why Me God?

"How in the hell did I get here?" I asked this question as if interviewing a familiar stranger. She looked a lot like me. She was me and I was her. Married too young, unequally yoked, bad credit, repossession, foreclosure, bankruptcy, divorce, unemployment and a diagnosis of an autoimmune disease. My bruises felt like hashtags I wore unceremoniously across my skin.

This wasn't supposed to be my story. I mean, I'm an educated, intelligent and strong woman, yet there I was: broke, homeless and unhappy. I was just shy of welcoming my 30th chapter when I found myself upside down and unsure of how I reached that destination. I had no idea that it was then, at that pivotal moment of low, my life transformation would began. I was separated from my ex-husband who had been my friend and my love and the man I created two precious daughters with. I was jobless and sleeping at my parents' home and driving a car from one of those buy-here-pay-here point A to B companies since my credit had reached its bottom too. In that place, I asked God what I'd done so wrong to deserve the condition of my life. What had I done?

My question hadn't fallen on deaf ears and God's response shook me in a way I'd never moved. He revealed to me that I'd become verbally abusive in my marriage;

throwing tantrums by lashing out and screaming with no obvious antecedent. It was as if evil energy jumped in my body and soul and came out through my lips in short increments of time and then dissipated just as quickly as it'd come. I'd revert back to my pre-tantrum mood and expect forgiveness and moving on to the next topic from my husband. I'm sure I appeared to be bipolar or suffering from some other mental illness when these incidents would occur. This behavior and over response to typical situations went on for nearly seven years. I expected forgiveness and understanding for my actions and moving on for almost 2,555 days. Constantly I was told that I had an issue, yet I seemed to be the only one that it didn't register with. I couldn't understand the war that was going on in my mind and claiming my communication.

    I never saw my conduct as being intentional, yet I was hell at home and heaven in public. Most saw me as a saint that was adored by many. Where was this underlying disease coming from then? Where and when had this inner aggression developed? Pain and heartache eventually lead me to peace. My therapist helped me understand wounds I obtained during childhood that never healed, yet aided in me becoming this horrible person who didn't know how to love.

    Once my marriage ended, I found myself there. Unhappy. Lost. My parents' roommate with my two daughters and no job… again. I cried every single day because I couldn't understand why my marriage had failed. Had my verbal aggression been so bad to cause the permanent divide between my husband and I? It took peeling back layers of my life through therapy to discover I'd come from a family of verbal abusers that probably had no idea that their actions were being sponged by my impressionable mind. Often we do as we see versus as we are told. We don't always recognize the influence of our familial surroundings until we catch ourselves doing exactly what they did that bothered us so much. I knew something was wrong in my life when I made this connection (I'd become them) and I knew that I desired to be happy. I desired to be completely opposite of how I'd become. It was as if God turned on a switch in my head and I got it. I got it! I was the only one who had the power to change what I didn't like about who I'd become and it was in that very moment that I made a decision that would turn out to be the best, most life-altering one. I made a decision to be intentional about the words I spoke, the company I kept *(removing negative people from my circle)* and finally loving myself.

Positive affirmations were spoken daily: Be strong, you got this, it's going to be okay. I knew I had to conquer my primary goals of getting myself back together. After all, I had two small children looking up to me and counting on me. They helped me pull out my inner strength and put my pieces back together again. Going through my divorce was like grieving a death in my life. I felt like it broke me, yet I know now that it was among my better decisions though it felt like the worst at the time. I'd never felt that kind of pain in my life. Looking back over things now though, I know that this is when it became obvious to me that God was moving in my life and opening doors that had been closed. I started applying for jobs and was fortunate enough to land a phone interview. After the season of sadness I'd been in, God showed me who he was when I was hired on the spot. I never met the woman who hired me, yet I know that it was

God in the midst of that call. I was thrilled to be offered the position as it gave me hope that this opportunity would help me get back where I needed to be, excel beyond where I'd been and start a new life.

Things were starting to work out in my favor, yet I knew I still needed help to propel me to where I was trying to go. A friend referred me to her life coach. I never known the role of a life coach, yet I was interested in learning more. Once I got more information, I was eager to receive her help though I knew I couldn't afford her. I made another great decision and invested in myself to become my best self. Little did I know, this awesome life coach would help me kick start the movement in transforming my life.

When I started working with her, I was lost as to how to move forward and love myself. She gave me specific self-care tasks to complete like reading the bible, getting massages regularly, getting my hair and nails done, eating healthy and working out. Prior to working with her, my daily routine had become: going to work, crying all day, picking up my children from school, eating dinner and then to bed five days a week. She encouraged me to enroll my children in afterschool twice weekly and to use that time to do something for me. Where there hadn't been time to do anything other than my normal routine, windows of time that belonged to me were opening up. I also hired a personal trainer that I worked out with two times per day on most days. My coach helped me advance in every area of my life. Initially, I was overweight, yet that year I lost 50 pounds. Her motivation and push was something I needed. She knew how to pour into me because she had also been through a divorce and turned her life around. I began to feel better about my life, though the hurt and pain hadn't completely gone away. I thought that after the divorce papers were signed, I would be better, yet the internal journey seemed to get worse.

    I continued working towards bettering myself, even though I was still mourning the loss of my marriage. One area that had caused a significant amount of stress in my life involved finances. I wanted to understand money better and the best ways to make smart financial decisions. I invested in a financial class at my church and it taught me how to change my mindset about money and how to best manage it. My financial situation had improved and was good, though I wasn't satisfied with the salary I was making while living in my hometown. I started applying for jobs in Atlanta and found one making $22,000 more than I was making at my job. I found a nice apartment for $1,200 per month which didn't seem expensive with the new salary I'd have. Life seemed to be looking up, yet as soon as I settled into the new position, a curveball came and I found myself in a low place again.

    I started the new job during the summer so my kids stayed with my parents until I could get settled and moved into my new place. The job was super demanding and I couldn't imagine handling it with my children living with me. On the 19th day in this new position, I entered the building as I usually did, however something was different. A spirit came over me and I heard God ask me, "why are you here?" The question was like confirmation of what I knew I had to do. I went to my manager, told her I could no longer do the job and I left. Here I was again, unemployed, now with a new apartment lease I'd just signed. I didn't know what I was going to do, yet when a friend asked if I was moving back home, I confidently said I was never going back. I trusted God enough to open another door and work it out. My faith was on an accelerated level.

I was hired for another position and I thought my life was looking up again. During my new employee training, I looked outside and saw that my car was being towed. I knew exactly what was happening, yet I had no idea of how to tell my manager, sitting right in front of me, that my car was being repossessed just outside the building. I had no choice but to be totally transparent. I told her what was happening and then ran outside to try and stop them. I was so humiliated and embarrassed. I had the money, but I'd been careless and had not paid the buy-here-pay-here company. Getting my car back caused me to have additional expenses that I didn't really have so I made another poor decision and got a title loan. They paid off the dealership, yet I had to pay the title company over double what I borrowed. In the midst of all this chaos, I was asked to leave my job because my performance wasn't what they expected it to be. I was surprised because I've never been asked to leave a job, though it was a release for me because of the stress I was dealing with. So, "here we go again," yet this time right before Christmas. The lesson and true purpose of this season was to praise God, not the holiday. Logically, I knew this, yet in the back of my mind, I was still asking God questions. Why me? Why am I going through so much?

I've grown to understand that you have not because you ask not. I felt like I had been pushed up against a wall with nowhere to turn or escape. It was then, in my apartment that I dropped to my knees in a cry out to God. I begged for him to help me and cried out my love for him. I was submitting to him. He somehow granted me mercy and favor. I'll never know why. God made a way for me from

December to March financially. I'm not sure exactly how, yet He did and I don't question it. It wasn't easy for me, yet I leaned on my faith and tried to remain positive. At the beginning of March, I received a call from a company asking if I was still in the market for a position. Eagerly I told them that I was. I interviewed for that position and was offered the job the same day. No words can truly express my excitement. I started wondering when I applied for this company and could not find anything connecting me to it. I had not applied for this position. God had moved in my life once again and once again, I was deeply grateful.

    I was excited for a chance to start over and went in with an optimistic mindset. I had hoped it'd be a new opportunity to grow and launch my career, though I couldn't have been more wrong. I felt like I stepped into hell when I started this job. The environment was negative and my manager wasn't the least bit supportive. I was reminded that not everyone in a position of leadership is actually called to lead. I decided to keep an armor of God's word around me and try to make the best out of it. I would listen to gospel music on the way to work, during work and on the way home just to get through my day. I was asking God, yet again, why me Lord?

    As the chaotic energy and drama continued and increased even with my staff, I started feeling like my spirit was missing something. I was thirsty for God. I needed him in a way I'd never known before. I decided to be baptized again in the name of the Father, the Son and the Holy Spirit which truly became the best decision I could've made in my life, for me as well as my family. I had a spirit of accountability over my life from that point on. Unfortunately, it didn't stop the pain and life trials, yet I did see my life differently. I now understood that the good and bad worked together for my good. I believe that everything that happens absolutely happens for a reason. In turn, God was using me to live out my purpose in life and be a blessing to others.

My prayers were coming to pass, though not the way I thought they would. It all happened in God's timing and His way. It was a process for me to understand that initially. Just when I least expected it, a blessing came my way. The manager's apartment became available at my job so I moved in and had free rent. I was also only 5-7 minutes away from my church. The apartment and location were both prayers to God that came to pass. This blessing allowed me to catch up on some debt, save and travel more. I think I took six different trips that year. I can honestly say that my quality of life improved greatly and that the office atmosphere at work changed for the better.

Without realizing it, I started stepping into my purpose. I used the ministry God gave me to do what was, at that time, just listening and talking to people as they experienced difficult life situations. I'd gone through so many tribulations that I wanted my journey to be a testimony I could share with people that may need to know they aren't alone in what they're dealing with. The more I ministered, the more people came to me. First it was at work only, then it was anyone God lead me to. He was molding me into a coach. I enjoyed helping people work through their life challenges. I wanted to be just like the person who came into my life and helped me transform. I started to seriously think about becoming a life coach. I prayed for God to send me clients and to use me in whatever way he felt he needed to.

Just like that, I had discovered my passion and life's purpose. I began helping women cultivate their vision by identifying meaningful goals that were S.M.A.R.T. (specific, measurable, attainable, realistic and timely) and creating action plans to aid in achieving better life fulfillment. Yes, I'd figured this thing called life out. I thought so anyway. Life was good, my credit had improved, I had money in the bank and had been pre-qualified to purchase another home. I had worked very hard to get to this point and I was enjoying the fruits of my labor.

Each time you take a step forward, something can happen that takes you some steps back. Just like almost any major storm we endure, I didn't see it coming. It started with stomach pain, nausea and diarrhea. I went back and forth to the doctor for a month, yet none of the medications worked. At one point, the pain became unbearable and I went to the hospital. After several tests and a week in the hospital, I was diagnosed with Ulcerative Colitis Disease. It's an autoimmune disease that affects the colon and the intestines of your body when inflamed. In order to keep the inflammation from happening, I have to have medical infusions done every eight weeks for the rest of my life. If not careful the medication can shut down all of my organs which can result in death. The disease is hereditary. My grandmother has it, I discovered, and at one point had to have a portion of her colon removed. It's similar to Crohn's Disease, yet not quite as severe. I asked the question again, why me God? I'm too young for something like this! Lord God, why me?

At this point in my life, I just trust God. I know and believe that all things, good and bad, work for the Glory of God. This disease was something I had to accept. I have learned to manage my condition and giving all glory to God, I have not had any more inflammation issues since being diagnosed three years ago.

Daily, I just thank God for keeping me in a good place even when things are imperfect. Yes, life throws you punches and curveballs and you're going to get knocked down. The question now is; will you stay down or are you going to rise above it all and deal with it? Many times, I could've stayed down and just given up, yet I knew I was supposed to be more because God kept telling me so. With all pain comes purpose. They say that the two most important days are the one in which you were born and the one in which you find out why. Knowing your why will help lead you to living your purpose. I understand who I am now, as a woman. I understand why I was born into this world. My purpose is to spread the word of Jesus Christ and help other women live the life they desire. Everything happens for a reason. We have to take the good with the bad and make it great. My prayer is that God continues to use me.

How's life now for me? Blessed. I finally completed my master's program and earned my MBA. I married my best friend last year and we have four beautiful children together. I'm a Real Estate Broker by profession and a Goal Strategist™ & Personal Coach by purpose. I love what I do and I'm looking forward to helping thousands more people become the best versions of themselves and find the answers to their why questions. Perhaps, I am that rose that grew right out the concrete of my pain, hurt, losses, failures and medical scares in order to become the woman I am today. I kept asking God; why me? His response is crystal clear now. Why not you? He only gives the most difficult battles to the

soldiers he knows will be resilient and make it through the storm victoriously. Well, call me victoriously grateful and blessed.
Blessings

Carnell Poteat

Carnell Poteat is a Veteran/Husband/Father/Writer who lives life to the fullest. His writings are inspired by his 6 years as Staff Sergeant in the Air Force, where he served as a Job Security Police. While enlisted, he secured his BA in Business Management and MS in Information Sciences from University of Phoenix. Carnell could be considered an ordinary guy with extraordinary imagination because he understands that there is nothing he cannot handle. The Sky is truly the limit!!

He is currently employed by the Department of Veteran Affairs, where he furthers his efforts and assists fellow Veterans and their dependents receive the benefits they deserve. On his spare time, you can find Carnell traveling, cooking, exercising and listening to various genres of music. Carnell is married with 3 children and currently lives in Wilmington, DE.

My August Angel

Who in your life could you say as extraordinary? I am not talking about money, fame, or possessions. Those are metrics that people sometimes use when illustrating somebody that they admire or appreciate. That perception is acceptable at times, but I do not consider those characteristics in most situations. Fortunately for me, I have had the luxury of meeting an extraordinary person. An individual who did not have much, but gave so much! This was in many forms to include wisdom, spirituality, and kindness. Occasionally, as I reflect on my own life I wonder what the meaning of life is truly. Why do we strive for things that will not matter when it is all over? I am thankful I was introduced to church and god from my mother. I think one person who possibly had it figured out was my mother. From time to time, I speculate if she was here to educate people about God. What I mean by that is she was a great friend by many because of her spirit. It was almost like she was an angel. My mother stayed true to herself in good and bad times. So, this story is about my mother and her experiences through my eyes. It may not be perfect, but I will try to piece together many accounts to show how she was exceptional.

    I was about 7 or 8 years old when I noticed that things were not quite right with my mother. What I mean by that is subtle changes in her personality started to appear. At this point she was struggling with four kids. My father would come around every so often, but it was not enough to call steady. So, she dealt with that as well as other tribulations. Growing up I believed I experienced too much and got disciplined frequently to being the oldest. I had issues with that growing up. I guess I wanted to be treated reasonably or like my siblings. She would tell me you are the oldest and you need to act like it. It was hard to comprehend then, but I understand it now. She wanted me to be a leader and a positive role model for my siblings. She was trying to instill this while growing up in the inner city of Wilmington, Delaware. She was trying to guide me to make the right decisions and not go along with things that would lead me to trouble. This was especially true with the daycare I was going to. This was a home daycare which the woman that ran it had sons about my age. Now at this point I did not know who they were, but I knew immediately that this was going to be a problem. Almost instantly I was a target. I say for about a year these two boys would bully me. I did not want to tell my mom because I knew she was struggling. So eventually I told my mother what was going on, but even after leaving the daycare I would still get bullied when I saw them around. Of course, my mom was angry about the situation, but not in the way you would think. I know she had to say something to the daycare owner, but she asked me, "What did I do? I am thinking, "what do you mean". I could not do anything as it was two against one. She said to me the words I still hear today with "Did you pray on it." I guess that was her way of saying God will protect you, but you need to seek him.

After living in a small apartment for our family, we eventually moved across town into a three-story house. At this point I was a teen and I was able to comprehend a little more. I also ended up running into those boys that bullied me previously. This time I just had the strength to stand up to them. I think after talking to my mother and praying about it I just said enough is enough. If we are going to fight then let's go. I am not afraid anymore. After me saying that, these boys did not want anything to do with me. It was like they saw something that they did not want to see. I credit that experience to my mother because she could have just handled it on her own without really talking to me but she wanted me to face my problems head on. Now I always thought of my mother as a strong person. I never saw anything that caused her to break. What I mean by that is she had us going to church and she would pray every day. She wanted our house to be sort of a sanctuary, but I had a hard time believing that as there were always situations going on in the house. Since being a very kind person, my mom was taken advantage of so many times. This was true when I was growing up. She would let random people stay with us because she just wanted to help. She was looking at the good and I was looking at the bad. For the most part, the situations ended well, but there were times where people would steal from us. It was very stressful growing up. It just seemed she attracted trouble. For example, she had a boyfriend who did drugs in the house. I even witnessed this while I was falling asleep. I really did not know what to do so I just froze. I was unable to go to sleep that night. I never told her about it because I did not want to add any stress.

  Our home was broken, at least for a period. There were so many issues that were happening I could not keep count. Along with the period with my mother dating, my father would show up occasionally which would proceed with arguments and fights. Previously, I remember being angry at everything and everyone. I was angrier at my father because I could not believe a man would treat a woman like that, especially my mother. Overall, I think she wanted the relationship to work as she kept taking him back and excusing his transgressions. I think that was the hard part for her. Trying to change somebody that did not want to change! This is where I started seeing changes mentally with her. Mental illness can truly take many forms and everybody is different. The factors and the circumstances are generally variable from person to person. It did not occur to me initially as a kid because I just thought it was a part of dealing with stress and situations. I also did not understand what was happening to my mother either. I considered her a strong-willed person, but as time went by that trait started diminishing.

  I got the full glimpse of her condition when I was in the military. It was while I was stationed in Wyoming when she would check on me constantly due to the wars in Iraq in Afghanistan. She was very paranoid watching the news around the clock. Generally, she was making sure my family and I were ok. My mom did not want me getting deployed either. Then I will say about half way into my six-year enlistment is when I received a phone call from my relatives stating she was missing. Missing, what are you talking about I asked. Initially I did not know what to think as so many bad thoughts were running through my head. This is when my aunt stated that I needed to get back home. The information I received was not complete and I was unable to paint a clear picture. I knew she had issues but I did not know the severity while being so far away. I later learned that my mom was located roaming the streets in a demented state. I ended taking extended time from the military to get more clarity. Overall, she was very good at hiding her condition from people until it hit the breaking point. Consequently, I ended speaking to doctors regarding her state and it was not good. The doctor told me that your mother has been diagnosed with Schizophrenia and Bipolar depression. She also looked malnourished like she had not eaten in weeks. It was a sad sight. I was thinking that this was not my mother. I was agreeing with the doctors that she needed to be medicated. I just wanted my mom back.

    Her condition and spirituality coincided with each other when off medication. During her episodes she could be seen praying in the middle the street barefooted. It was like she was in a different time during her spells. Often, we would travel miles around the city searching for her. It became a regular occurrence. Generally, I was afraid that somebody would try to harm her. When talking to her after she was stabilized, she still was not afraid. Habitually, I pondered if my message to her was correct. I was just repeating the doctor's orders. Maybe she had things figured out and we did not. I knew something was not right because she would forget about everything during her spells. She would just pray for god to come get her. I thought, why was she trying to leave. Maybe she fulfilled her purpose in this life and it was time for the next chapter. The best I could describe her condition was the classic fight between good and evil. It was like seeing someone possessed at times. As her episodes became more frequent, I once asked my mother if she contemplated suicide. There was a slight pause as if I stumbled onto something. Always thought my mother would not commit such an act as she was a god-fearing woman. It just made me wonder if she has given up this time. After years and years of fighting this illness her symptoms were starting to get the best of her. She was not functioning the way we were accustomed to. Throughout it all, she stayed kind and respectful of others. She was always a good listener. Probably a key moment for me is when I told my mother about my son. When he was about two years old, he was having seizures which were very traumatic for us. He ended up being diagnosed with epilepsy and put on daily medication. I told my mother that I researched omega 3 or fish oil supplements for his condition. There was a lot of research regarding brain development so me and my wife decided to give it try for his seizures. After that, he eventually grew out of the condition and never had a seizure since. My mom stated that was the grace of God and I agreed. It was a trying time for my family and I always believed we would get through it. Then about a month after telling my mom that story I went to her house to visit. As I walked in the house, I noticed boxes upon boxes of supplements. Most of them were omega 3 fish oil. I am not big into crying but I could not hold back the tears as she was willing to try anything to get back to normal. I mean I just told her a story about what we did, but I do not know if it truly worked.

Over the years I witnessed my mother grow weaker and weaker. She still was quoting scriptures and dancing around the house to gospel music, but I knew that these days were different. I would get calls frequently from family members stating that I needed to check on my mom. Even though I knew it would be a battle, I would always try to reach out and get her back to normal. It was frustrating because she was very good at manipulating the system. It was almost comical sometimes how she would toy with us during her episodes. This was especially true when I went over to her house during a spell. I called the authorities to take her to the hospital for a mental evaluation. Prior to the authorities arriving at her home, my mother was dancing around yelling out scriptures of the bible. Again, she has not eaten for weeks and she needed medical attention. Her weight was dangerously low. So, when the officers arrived, my mother came downstairs somewhat coherent and said "What is the problem, I'm fine" "Why did you call these people over here." At this point the authorities were looking at me like I was crazy and I told them she is on file, take her. It was like she flipped a switch to go back to normal for a minute. After that, the officers left because they did not see her as a threat to others, but it is ok to look sick. I was very angry at this point and I just left. I later laughed it off because she fooled all of us. I guess I was just glad she was in her house this time. I have learned throughout this process that it is hard to get somebody committed if they are not a threat to others. Often it was a constant circle of going to the hospital, receiving therapy, and getting released.

    The real problem I would say is that we did not fully understand my mother's issues. She would talk to counselors and people she did not know sometimes but refused to elaborate with her family. We would get bits and pieces of information but it was not enough to help us figure things out. Generally, it was a combination of factors. Circumstances that may not be known since she was so secretive! As I said before, she was great at listening and resolving other people's problems, but not her own. I do not think it was one event that caused her schizophrenia and bi-polar depression. It was a gradual buildup of situations which she did not properly address. Throughout the years and years of trying to get her better this was our new normal. I would anticipate my mother having an episode each week because it was so frequent. Her counselors assured me it was the lack of medication, but at this point I was just lost. I felt like she was being taken over and one day we will lose her forever. Unfortunately, that thought came to fruition when I was called to her house for the very last time. This time I was frustrated as usual. My mother was not completely gone so I tried to get her to take her medication. She also was trying to leave. I told her that if this keeps happening you will go into a long-term facility for good. I knew that was a stretch but I was just trying to get her to take her medication. So, I ended up leaving because I could not do any more. After a few days I received a call that my mother was missing again. She left her home again to walk the streets. This time was different though. Normally she would show up in one of the hospitals around the city within a day or two. This was not the case, as some of my family members were concerned. We were still hopeful that she would show up like she always has. I just remember this time being sick to my stomach because something was not right.

It was uncanny, and felt like she was already gone because I had a dream where I just saw her face. I woke up soon after that and started crying. I felt like I always had a connection with her and that was another example. Her coming to me in my dream was reassurance that she was ok. Afterwards, my thoughts were confirmed when I received a call from my family stating a body was found in the Delaware River. I was at work when I received the information and I could not keep it in any longer. I started to cry because her life ended traumatically. We did not know the full circumstances besides that she may have drowned.

Throughout this ordeal, my uncle stated her birthday came out straight on the day lottery. Her birthday was August 16. This was also the day we were notified of her death. The lottery was another message that gave me comfort in her passing. I just wished I could have wrapped my arms around her to say *"I love you"* before she left. My mother had just turned 50 in August and she told me after her birthday, "I made it to 50." I still wonder what she meant by that. Did she plan this? Was she tired of being trapped in her own mind? There are still so many questions and not enough answers. Overall, I have learned a lot from my "August Angel". As I reflect on her life, I've gained more insight on what I need to do in my own life. I need to help others and give back! This is what she did every day. She was a wonderful person with flaws just like everyone else, but the fact that she always treated people kindly is something I can respect and live for. I still believe today that she is watching and praying over us. This is why I try to live my life to not disappoint my angel in heaven.

Tyressa Ty

From the Tom Joyner Cruise, to Brian McKnight, and now Doug E. Fresh, Celebrity Host Tyressa Ty is one of the hottest and fastest rising people in the industry.

Tyressa (tī-rē-să) known as Tyressa Ty, is a native of Louisiana. She is a graduate of Southern University and A&M College, and The University of Phoenix. Tyressa has a Bachelor of Arts degree in Mass Communications and a Master of Business Administration degree with a Marketing concentration; and she also holds a Professional Human Resources Certificate. Tyressa Ty is currently a Corporate Trainer for one of the largest telecommunications companies in the United States. She has over ten years of Media, Sales

& Marketing, and Public Relations experience, specializing in Radio and Television.

She has hosted big name events all over the country and was the announcer heard on the first session of Mary Mary's WeTv Reality Show. Additionally, she has conducted up close and personal interviews with big names like New Orleans Saints', Tracey Porter, Harry Connick, Jr., Bobby Brown, Keith Sweat, Matthew Knowles (Beyoncé's Father) and Pooch Hall, to name a few. She was also the key reporter for Essence Fest Gospel featuring Kim Burrell, Yolanda Adams, Donnie McCurklin, and Alexis Spight.

Of all her accomplishments, Tyressa is most proud of being the mom of her son. Tyressa attends Living Faith Christian Center and a proud member of Delta Sigma Theta Sorority, Incorporated.

Contact Info:
Website: https://www.tyressaty.com/

Forging through the "Fiyah"

Everyone has challenges to overcome. However, when you look at what Tyressa Ty has, is, and continues to fight and forge through, it really makes you wonder how she can handle the fiyah.

She lives through the challenges of being a single mother/parent.

She survives the ordeal of Hurricane Katrina where she loses everything, and I do mean EVERYTHING from home to other possessions. That alone would be enough, but there's more adversity she is working through that would make many decide to quit, let alone wonder why.

She lost her home due to the floods in Baton Rouge; in fact, given the hurricane in 2016, this makes two times where her home and livelihood have been destroyed in a more than devastating manner.

Somehow, she still goes forward through the fiyah.

Why? How?

If a testimony is a test, then she's clearly been and is being testing beyond anyone's comprehension. Again, where others would have long since fallen off or given up, someway, somehow, be it swift or slow, she keeps moving forward. Despite the challenges of home, family, and health, she's somehow still here. Despite living from place to place due to her housing situation, she is still doing what she can.

Ranging from the work she does now as the brand manager for Doug E. Fresh, to hosting events including the Tom Joyner Cruise and others, she is considered one of the hardest working and fastest rising figures in the entertainment industry. Given the work through her book Follow the Fiyah: For Ordinary People Chasing Extraordinary Dreams, she motivates, uplifts, and encourages others to find their passion and purpose, even in the midst of setbacks and life challenges. In fact, her book is required reading for the Baton Rouge (LA) Community College Chapter of Upward Bound/Trio; add to it her ongoing work with #DivasAndDolls, she provides self-esteem and self-image enhancement for young girls of color.

How does she forge through the "fiyah", and how can others do so?

Fanning the flames is one way; remember the reason why you started on your journey (be it professional, community, or personal) in the first place and stay the course. **Turn up the heat** as at times, you have to turn up your energy level; get started on getting things underway, as well as identify things you need to stop doing in order to get to where you need to go. At times, the **fiyah escape** is needed in the form of escape, outside, and inside. At times, you have to work your backup plan, adjust your current plan, get some help or assistance on a matter, as well as create some personal time and space to simply reboot or pause and get things together. Likewise, remembering some essential rules such as (but not limited to) remembering who you are and whose you are, knowing your passion and purpose, remaining humble, learning to laugh and laugh hard, and knowing your worth are things that we all can do and do consistently, even in the midst of life's trials and tribulations.

Yes, even the strongest of us needs a lift and word of encouragement and empowerment. In the midst of it all, she is able to remain spiritually grounded, focused, passionate, enlightening, energetic, full of humor, and full of positive energy for others to build upon, let alone feed and fuel the "fiyah" within.

This is her story, let alone what she does in going above and beyond.

Notes

COMPILED BY

CHARRON MONAYE

Award-winning playwright/author/coach/entrepreneur and writer, Charron Monaye is living the life she prayed for. Using her extraordinary gifts, Charron has developed a following among aspiring entrepreneurs and writers who seek her knowledge and life lessons on an array of subjects.

Since 2011, Charron Monaye has authored eight books, co-authored two books, and wrote/produced three theatrical productions. She is a former content contributor for CNN News iReport and The Philadelphia Association of Paralegals. Understanding the importance of reaching back and helping others achieve their goals, she has made it her mission to help other entrepreneurs build their businesses and publishing goals through her company, Pen Legacy®, LLC.

Charron has a Bachelor's of Arts in Political Science from West Chester University, Master's in Public Administration from Keller Graduate School of Management, a Certificate in Paralegal Studies and Life Coaching, and a Doctorate of Philosophy (Humane Letters) from CICA International University & Seminary. Charron is a member of Zeta Phi Beta Sorority, Inc., Order of Eastern Star and First Baptist Church of Crestmont.

Contact Info:
Company Website: www.penlegacy.com
Author Website: www.charronmonaye.com
Email: info@penlegacy.com
Facebook & Twitter: PenLegacy
Instagram: iamcharronmonaye
LinkedIn: Charron Monaye, MPA

SHONTAYE HAWKINS, MPA

Known as the Bottom Line Strategist™, Shontaye Hawkins, MPA uses her extensive finance background and financial prowess to equip small business owners with the knowledge and strategies to build highly profitable businesses. During her career with Fortune 500 companies such as Goldman Sachs® and Bank of New York®, she worked with top business leaders to build wealth in excess of $1 billion and attract high net worth clients. Shontaye has been a Fox News Radio contributor along with being a featured guest expert on CBS Radio, Black Enterprise and along with many other media outlets across the country.

As a Business Coach, Author, Speaker and CEO & Founder of Profit Is The New Black®, Shontaye teaches her clients practical strategies to keep their profits in the black – making money and achieve the financial success they desire and deserve. Shontaye says, "It doesn't take money to make money. It takes action."

Contact Info:
Shontaye Hawkins
www.ProfitIsTheNewBlack.com
shontaye@profitisthenewblack.com
Facebook – www.Facebook.com/ShontayeHawkinsCoaching
Twitter - ShontayeH
LinkedIn – ShontayeHawkins

Motivate and Inspire Others
Order More Copies

Retail Price $19.99

Special Quantity Discounts

5-20 Books	$17.95 each
21-99 Books	$15.95 each
100-499 Books	$12.95 each
500-999 Books	$9.95 each
1000+ Books	$6.95 each

To Place An Order Contact:
info@penlegacy.com
or Your Favorite Contributing Co-Author

www.ingramcontent.com/pod-product-compliance
Lightning Source LLC
Chambersburg PA
CBHW071928290426
44110CB00013B/1528